THE POET *and* THE MACHINE

THE

POET

AND THE

MACHINE

by PAUL GINESTIER

TRANSLATED FROM THE FRENCH BY MARTIN B. FRIEDMAN

CHAPEL HILL

THE UNIVERSITY OF NORTH CAROLINA PRESS

Contents

Translator's Note

THE POET AND THE MACHINE, which marks Paul Ginestier's introduction to English-speaking readers, is the result of the application to the study of contemporary poetry of a method employed by the author in several volumes dealing with various branches of literature and whose general title is "Toward a Science of Literature." Discarding mere biographical discussion which forms so large a part of traditional critical analysis, Dr. Ginestier demonstrates how frequently a poem can be illuminated by the discoveries of the pre-eminent modern sciences, psychoanalysis and sociology, in a study whose thematic unity—the influence upon poetry of the material progress of society—offers coherent and exciting evidence of the importance of his new approach. The information which he brings to bear upon the critical task compliments the techniques of traditional criticism, and the results demonstrate the truth of Dr. Ginestier's formula that "whatever sheds light upon life sheds light upon literature."

The translations of French poetry quoted in the text are intended to assist the reader to an understanding of the original passages, but the complexity of many of these precludes any translation from furnishing a precise equivalent of the original; consequently, the author's argument can best be understood if the English version is employed as a guide to the French, and not as a substitute for it, whenever such help is needed. To this end the translations have been made line by line as far as was possible. One or two passages were left untranslated for obvious reasons.

This translation has been done in close co-operation with the author, who has provided much new material of interest to an English-speaking audience, and whose generous assistance has relieved his translator of a great part of that constant concern that his expression may fall far short of being a faithful reproduction of the original thought. The entire manuscript was carefully read and many helpful suggestions were offered by Professor Alfred G. Engstrom of the University of North Carolina, to whom the translator is indebted for efforts which amounted at times almost to collaboration. To Professor Engstrom, and to the staff of The University of North Carolina Press, are due many improvements in this book, and to them, and to Amelia Milch, for a faultlessly prepared typescript, goes my grateful appreciation. Finally, I wish to thank the authors and publishers of the works quoted for the use of their material in these pages.

MARTIN B. FRIEDMAN

New Haven, Connecticut

January 3, 1961

THE POET *and* THE MACHINE

1.

Outline for a Method of Literary Aesthetics

LITERARY CRITICISM today has been shaken by a storm comparable to that which raged over Victor Hugo's *Hernani* in 1830 and gave rise to a new theater, or to the momentous influence of Symbolism which produced such far-reaching consequences for poetry. On one side are the conservatives who hold to a strict application of the historical method as "the prince of critics," Sainte-Beuve, defined it: "I have often heard modern criticism, and my own in particular, reproached for being entirely historical, entirely individual. . . . Literature, literary production, is not distinct or separable, for me, from the rest of man. . . . I can enjoy a work of art, but I find it difficult to judge it independently of a knowledge of the man himself. I would say willingly: as the tree, so is the fruit."[1] On the other side are the revolutionaries who recommend silent admiration of masterpieces, grouping themselves behind Paul Claudel, who remarked, "The most beautiful is that which you will not understand,"[2] and Paul Valéry, who wrote in his "Préface à Adonis," "Everything that history can observe is insignificant."[3]

It seems to us, however, that between the meticulous observation of the rituals of historical method and the admir-

1. Charles-Augustin Sainte-Beuve, *Nouveaux Lundis*, III.
2. "Première journée," *Le Soulier de satin* (Paris: Gallimard, 1929), p. 18.
3. *Variété* (Paris: Gallimard, 1924), p. 81.

ing silence of the new Quakers of literature, there is room for a method at once more flexible and more thorough. The aesthetician confronted with a masterpiece does not exclude *a priori* any system of explication but tries to make a synthesis of all the means of investigation which the present state of knowledge offers him. This absence of a preconceived idea allows him to reconsider the problem of literary criticism and to take it up again at its foundation, thus rediscovering a prime definition which may be developed into a very useful syllogism:

> Language = a succession of symbols.
> Literature = a superior form of language.
> ∴ Everything which helps to shed light upon the symbol and its source sheds light upon literature.

Two modern sciences—the sociology of primitive life and psychoanalysis—are devoted to the elucidation of human symbols and thus become privileged instruments of aesthetic literary criticism. The weakness of these sciences is that they lend themselves easily to ridicule. As often happens, those who make fun of them attack characteristics which, in fact, do not belong to the disciplines arraigned. They reproach the sociologists who show an interest in primitive humanity with wanting "to make us walk on all fours," as Voltaire wrote to Rousseau, August 30, 1755; but is there the least analogy between the idealized depiction of the first man in *The Social Contract* and an organized systematic study of primitive customs such as *The Golden Bough?*[4] In the same way psychoanalysis is stigmatized because it grants too large a place to the libido, and thus becomes an easy mark for irony, e.g., supposing "The Ancient Mariner" to be a poem resulting from unsatisfied sexual desires, our gratitude for this masterpiece ought to go to the puritan Mrs. Coleridge.

4. Sir James Frazer, *The Golden Bough: A Study in Magic and Religion*, 12 vols. (New York: Macmillan, 1905-15). Also in abridged one-volume edition (New York: Macmillan, 1922), hereafter cited.

This is naturally based on a confusion between psychoanalytic method and the doctrine of Freud, two quite different things, as Roland Dalbiez has shown in a fine book, *La Méthode psychanalytique et la doctrine freudienne.*[5]

Finally, certain critics, having surrendered in spite of rooted prejudices, accept the aesthetic method only as a stopgap. They consent to make use of the light shed by the new sciences, but only when the historical method and logical explication have failed. They postulate a fundamental contradiction between the image and the idea. If, as Sartre has shown,[6] the image is neither "a colorless perception" nor "a concept" but constitutes "a certain kind of consciousness," if it is "an act and not a thing," it should not be more remote from existential logic than the rest of psychic life. Evidently, in thought, logic reveals itself in a pure state at the level of concepts, while in imagination it is hidden at the deeper level of articulated symbols. It is a question of a logic of relations[7] and not of a rigid logic of modes.

Moreover, there is no clearly determined distinction. Every thought contains images, and every thing imagined contains a thought, however elementary it may be. At the human level, pure thought and pure imagination do not exist. We believe that every life unfolds according to a psychic current, and that it is vain to dogmatize by calling one or another method exclusively correct, because an incompatibility of methods presupposes an incompatibility of objects, and it cannot be said that different moments in a single psychic life are incompatible.

And since all human beings have bodies that are similar in their general aspects, why should not their psyches be likewise similar to all others? Certainly, irreducible dif-

5. (Paris: Desclée de Brouwer, 1936).

6. Jean-Paul Sartre, *L'Imagination* (Paris: Presses Universitaires de France, 1949), p. 162.

7. As defined by Charles Serrus, "La logique des relations et les deux degrés de la logique" in *Essai sur la signification de la logique* (Paris: Alcan, 1939).

ferences exist in the details, but it is wise to follow the method of the organic sciences and concentrate on the substance rather than on the modifications of it.   Good sense, according to the Cartesian definition, is the common yardstick of human thoughts.   The archetype occupies a similar position with regard to human imagination.   According to Jung, archetypes or primordial images are "the psychic residua of numberless experiences of the same type."[8] Frances Wickes, in a more recent work, observes, "No one is born a new being.   He bears in his psyche the imprint of past generations."[9]   This theory is accepted by the majority of modern psychologists.   It is proven by the fact that we constantly recreate images that our ancestors had invented. As La Bruyère remarked in the Preface to *Les Caractères ou les moeurs de ce siècle* (1688): "Everything has been said and we have arrived too late, since men have been thinking for more than seven thousand years."   There is nothing but inventing things all over again.   I would like to add only one example which was offered me recently. My eight-year-old son, after seeing a drawing of an octopus in a magazine, asked, "The tentacles grow back after they've been cut off, don't they?   What do they call it when an octopus has a head at the end of each tentacle?"   No one had ever talked to him about mythology, and he did not suspect that he had just rediscovered the Hydra of Lerna.

Archetypes are thrown into society in much the same way as men.   Some remain obscure and live out a humble existence; others, much less numerous, become famous and are called myths.   Humanity has been conscious of their existence since time immemorial, and the influence of Greek mythology on western civilization is well known.   The imaginary world ruled by Zeus is as familiar today as it

8. Carl G. Jung, *Contributions to Analytical Psychology* (New York: Harcourt, Brace & Co., 1928), p. 246.

9. *The Inner World of Man* (New York: Farrar & Rinehart, 1938), p. 50.

was in the seventeenth century, but it is regarded in a very different way. In the classical period the approach was poetical and historical, while today it is social and psychoanalytic. The quip, "Oedipus was probably the only one who didn't know about the complex that bears his name," illustrates very well the interest mythologies still offer us. They are documents which precede any doctrine of the subconscious and are therefore exempt from the sort of conditioning that is likely to deform any scientific experiment in this field.

It is just that, in fact, which constitutes the most serious objection to the purely psychoanalytic method of interpreting modern texts. There is no way of distinguishing with certainty between true introspection or dream transcription, and the application of a handbook on the subject. Nothing prevents an unscrupulous writer or poet desiring to lay a trap from starting, for example, with a chapter of Freud and inventing symbols. The critic who afterwards falls into ecstasies over the Freudian meaning of such work, assuming a persuasive coincidence between the theoretical and the real, where there is nothing but logical application of a text and artificial invention of facts, will obviously be taken in. And this is so much like a literary swindle that one would almost be tempted to conclude with the famous formula of Jules Romains' Monsieur Le Trouhadec (who, to save his reputation as a geographer and professor at the Sorbonne, accepts a student's offer to create the town of Donogoo in South America—a town which the professor had unwittingly invented and described at length in a scholarly work of geography): "All science, Monsieur . . . rests on a foundation of trust."[10]

But it is still true that modern poets have been profoundly influenced by Freud and his disciples. André Breton, the pope of surrealism, studied Freudian doctrine

10. *Donogoo* (Paris: Gallimard, 1930), p. 50.

as early as 1915 when he was attached to the neuro-psychiatric center of the French army. Seventeen years later, in *Les Vases communicants*, he cites a revealing passage from Freud: "[Poets] are masters of us ordinary men, in knowledge of the mind, because they drink at streams which we have not yet made accessible to science. Why has the poet not spoken out even more clearly for nature, full of meanings and dreams?"[11]   In the same way, one of the greatest contemporary poets, W. H. Auden, dedicates a poem "In Memory of Sigmund Freud." Here are two of the twenty-eight stanzas:

> But he would have us remember most of all
> to be enthusiastic over the night
>> Not only for the sense of wonder
>> It alone has to offer, but also
>
> Because it needs our love: for with sad eyes
> Its delectable creatures look up and beg
>> Us dumbly to ask them to follow;
>> They are exiles who long for the future[12]

It is remarkable to see the best critical discussion devoted to this poet, Richard Hoggart's *Auden: an Introductory Essay*, return twenty-one times to psychoanalysis as a theme of inspiration.[13]

Confronted by these proofs of an enthusiasm which is approved by most modern poets, we are obliged to consider the possibility of a sort of unconscious osmosis by which the modern writer may model his work according to Freudianism and thus cause an interpretation based on the same philosophy to be nothing more than an outline of principles, without critical value. Many critics are aware of this problem. A first attempt at a solution consists in studying, to begin with,

---

11. (Paris: Editions des Cahiers libres, 1932), p. 128.
12. *The Collected Poetry of W. H. Auden* (New York: Random House, 1945).
13. (New Haven: Yale University Press, 1951).

only texts earlier than 1900 (date of the first publication of Freud's *The Interpretation of Dreams*), and then to profit in some way from the facility acquired to enter briefly into the twentieth century. This is what has been done in two excellent works, Maud Bodkin's *Archetypal Patterns in Poetry*[14] and F. L. Lucas' *Literature and Psychology*.[15] These authors count on literary relationships to support the Freudian interpretations they give of modern texts.

A second method, which rests on broader bases, consists in putting psychoanalysis within a system of literary aesthetics in which the dominant idea may be one like that of time (Georges Poulet),[16] or a system like that of the economy of passions (Charles Lalo),[17] or even that metaphysic of the imagination founded on the four elements proposed by Bachelard.[18] Like all trail-blazers, these authors have been passionately discussed, but they constitute a united front because they complement, without contradicting, one another. They are accused especially of deferring to an ephemeral fashion and of aiming at celebrity by a demagogic appeal to the public at large, which is always eager for novelties. But do they really follow the fashion, or do they carry it progressively forward?

Freudianism, which constituted a major intellectual revolution, appealed also to the general public because it happened to give a kind of scientific excuse for the libidinous. Of course its popularizers did not fail to place the system on a moral plane, for which it was not intended, and to sing its praises, endowing its explanations with the value of justifica-

14. (London: Oxford University Press, 1934).

15. (Ann Arbor: University of Michigan Press, 1957).

16. *Studies in Human Time* (Baltimore: The Johns Hopkins Press, 1956) and *The Interior Distance* (Baltimore: The Johns Hopkins Press, 1959).

17. *L'Art et la vie*, 3 vols. (Paris: J. Vrin, 1942).

18. Gaston Bachelard, *La Psychanalyse du feu* (Paris: Gallimard, 1949); *L'Eau et les rêves* (Paris: J. Corti, 1942); *L'Air et les songes* (Paris: J. Corti, 1943); *La Terre et les rêveries du repos* (Paris: J. Corti, 1948); *La Terre et les rêveries de la volonté* (Paris: J. Corti, 1948).

tions. This fashion was defined with ironical clarity by Paul Valéry: ". . . there is no person of refinement who does not dredge up, every morning, from his very depths some abysmal monstrosities, some polyps of an obscene shape, which he marvels at himself for having bred." Further on in the same letter, he gives an admirable definition: "Myths are the souls of our actions and of our loves. We can act only by moving toward a phantom. We can love only that which we ourselves create."[19] This subtle definition explains the present popularity of myths: they associate themselves with the anti-intellectual movement which characterizes our era. Overwhelmed by the immense technical progress due to scientific reason and the methodical application of the intelligence, we seek to recover our psychic equilibrium and, by a common process of compensation, we have a tendency to magnify all that seems to escape the intellect. The more man becomes civilized in practice, the more he wants to return to the primitive in theory. The cults of nature and camping correspond to our taste for the irrational and to the attraction exercised by the most mysterious sciences. Thus the present popularity of the myth corresponds to a collective need rather than to a romantic infatuation. Sociologists would be wrong to neglect the study of these tendencies, for they constitute an important symptom of the sickness of our times.

When there are a large number of individuals in a society, they develop adaptive mental processes for its spiritual context which channel their psychic dynamism into similar directions. It is curious to notice that the existence of a collective mode of thinking may be accepted as a commonplace, while the existence of a collective mode of imagining is considered a paradox. It would seem, in effect, that reverie is above all an intimate pleasure, and that men hold to it as the ultimate proof of the independence of their ego.

19. "Petite lettre sur les mythes" in *Variété II* (Paris: Gallimard, 1930), p. 223.

But the truth is more brutal. *Give me a woman and a fish and I will imagine a mermaid* is only the particular instance of *give me A and B and I will imagine C.* Now it happens that the factors A and B are for the most part similar for all men; hence the common proportion of all imagined C's. This does not mean uniformity. We all know that there is a difference between Malherbe and Rimbaud, but it is true of imaginations as it is of triangles: their variety is infinite, but they have common properties.

The most important of these is, in our opinion, the ambivalence which reigns at all levels of mental life and of which Pascal, that great imagination, gives us many examples. Consequently, if our classic example A, B, and C is true and indicates that imagination is the function of the real—in the sense that images are made by a combination of bits of reality—it does not exclude the fact that it is also the function of the unreal—in the sense that such a combination has no actual existence except in our minds and, if we are true artists, in our works. "Our thought moves toward reality; it does not spring from it."[20] Thus we have a dialectic between our psyche and the world. Now, since poetry is an art which exercises all the faculties of the individual, it is not possible to treat the psychic side of the creator partially. But the subject is so vast that it is necessary to subdivide it. It is clear that only as the imagination makes use of things of the world can it be examined; hence the major reason for the study of themes. This method, revealing the reactions of numerous poets before a common object, ought to allow us, by multiplying the evidence, to avoid those analyses which are the mere outlines of principles we mentioned above.

Certainly, monographic studies in the true Sainte-Beuve tradition have great value. Based on a profound knowledge of an author and his work, they throw a considerable light on his psychic current and his creative genius, as well as on

20. Gaston Bachelard, *La Valeur inductive de la rélativité* (Paris: J. Vrin, 1929), p. 241.

the world that they reflect. Moreover, Montaigne's words have lost none of their merit: "Every man carries within him the entire form of the human condition." At the same time, only a comparative literature can show us in what measure such an extension to the artist as a man is legitimate; only a study of the treatment of each theme can allow us to distinguish between whimsical and permanent characteristics in the dialectic of the imagination. In addition, it is necessary to remain aware of the reality of facts. Every text implies a double origin, first at the level of him who conceives, but also—and this is too often forgotten—at the level of him who receives. The imagination is a sort of shuttle which cannot, in fact, weave literature until it has completed three movements:

> From the poet to the world—From the world to the poet
> From the poet to the poem—From the poem to the reader
> From the reader to the world—From the world to the reader

And although many authors make a pretense of disdaining the last phase, it is, in our opinion, every bit as important as the others.

Thus we find ourselves directed toward a triangular study: world, psychology of the imagination (poet and reader), and literary appreciation of a poem. Although we consider this aesthetic essential, it is evident that any exposition would be more convincing if we could find, in theory, a governing principle existing on two of the three lines of investigation. The interrelation between the world and our psychic lives is such that we have a wide range of choices. It seems to us, however, that the principle of power merits special attention. The dream of power, which precedes that of force, is one of the most salient characteristics of dream work. Examples abound to show that this notion

is the epicenter of our imaginary life. Like the simple milk-
maid in the fable who has visions of the fortune that will
grow from her jug of milk, we all, at certain times, dream of
a victorious superiority. The best moments are those in
which nothing is impossible to us, when our mind abandons
our body to wander in a world of fantasy. To this is due the
irresistible attraction of drugs such as opium and cocaine
which permit the person under their influence to create these
dreams at will. For the same reason, all mythologies are
full of heroes and gods who actualize man's dream of power;
the alchemical philosopher's stone, panacea, and elixir of
long life are merely objectifications of imaginary power.
Quite naturally force, especially in the form of war, has been
introduced into numerous poetical expressions like the
Chansons de Geste. The song of praise for the conqueror
has a significance which transcends the events themselves;
through it the poet identifies himself with the victory and
the reader participates in it.

All this corresponds closely to the fact that force is also of
major importance on the social level. It is enough to recall
the famous remarks, among a thousand others, of La Fontaine
("la raison du plus fort") and of Bismarck ("might is
superior to right"). In politics peace has always been the
result of a balance of forces, war the result of an imbalance,
most often imaginary. Many wars have been unleashed
because a state *imagined* it was the strongest when, in
reality, a long decline had brought it into a position of
equilibrium with others. Bertrand Russell has demonstrated
in a remarkable book that "the fundamental concept in
social science is Power, in the same sense in which Energy
is the fundamental concept in physics."[21] One of the greatest
events of human history has been the industrial revolution
which multiplied the physical forces at our disposal. There
is, manifestly, a basic concept here which can serve as a point

21. *Power: A New Social Analysis* (New York: W. W. Norton & Co.,
1938), p. 12.

of reference. Statisticians have found a convenient means of establishing the industrial level of a nation. If every worker of a certain country disposes of two horsepower of energy, while the corresponding figure for another nation is four horsepower, they conclude that the second is twice as well-developed as the first, and this conclusion, although approximate, cannot be far from the truth.

Now it happens that we have had an upsetting, or rather a revolutionary enrichment, of the concept of imagination corresponding to the advent of the machine age. Although the imagination was frequently conceived by writers of the last century to be an organizing power operating on the visible world, it has become, for contemporary thinkers, a living part of the psychic dynamism. C. Baudouin expresses this in a luminous manner: "Psychoanalysis has undertaken to disclose that dreams are the brothers of actions; it has reestablished them in the current of life; it has thus restored their value."[22]

This process has been carried as far as possible, and it has even been affirmed that an image must necessarily produce its realization (ontogenesis). One of the most striking theories of our time, that of Bachelard, underlines the prevalence of the classical four elements in the world, the psyche, and practically all the data of the imagination. The four elements do seem to "exist" universally in the realm of the myth,[23] since they are to be found simultaneously in alchemy, cosmology, the signs of the zodiac, the rivers of Hell, medicine, anatomy, etc. As a kind of *a posteriori* illustration, T. S. Eliot bases his *Four Quartets*[24] on earth, water, air, and fire.

In our opinion, there is a revolution here which has put an end to the divorce which, for a very long time, has

22. *De l'instinct à l'esprit* (Bruges: Desclée de Brouwer, 1950), p. 76.
23. Cf. *Psychology and Alchemy* in Herbert Read, ed., *The Collected Works of C. G. Jung*, XII (New York: Pantheon, 1954).
24. (New York: Harcourt, Brace, 1943).

separated the imagination from the world. Like an old married couple, they lived side by side through habit, and with no other contact than a degrading routine. Thanks to the new theories, showing how the development of the imagination conforms to the laws of development in the material world, they are rediscovering one another. An affection which they never suspected is taking hold of them, and at last they can be used to elucidate those problems of poetic creation which concerned them, not separately, but as a true couple.

One of the consequences of this metaphysic of the imagination is the manner in which it affects time, transforming it into a rhythmic continuity, not by which we live, but which in itself lives, since it is an integral part of us. This analysis of rhythm is one of the great efforts of criticism in our century, and it has, in turn, helped to restore lost values. In the words of Gaston Bachelard: "Poetry, thus liberated from habitual influences, became again a model of life and rhythmed thought."[25]

It is important to note that one of the essential characteristics of the machine age is precisely the imposition of a mechanical rhythm upon the *laissez-faire* of the organic periods in which man was closer to his origins. One of the great factors of today's poetical creation results from the conflicts and problems of adjustment which have developed out of the superimposition of a metallic rhythm upon the psychic rhythm.

We do not propose to make an exercise of applying these theories. They do play, however, an important role in the eclecticism of our aesthetic method, and we think that, applied carefully, without excluding the more classic procedures, they help us to appreciate a literary work in a more lucid manner.

We think that, in everyday life, imagination precedes

25. *La Dialectique de la durée* (Paris: Boivin, 1936), p. 170.

action in a more or less distinct manner; in what are called spontaneous acts it happens that the imaginative process has not been conscious or has been forgotten. There would be much to gain, and nothing to lose, by studying the speeches of *Le Cid*, for example, from the viewpoint of the development of an imagination which culminates in the words, "Courons à la vengeance," leading to a subsequent action.

But the ties are even closer, since to a simple succession may be added an influence of imagination upon action, which serves either to magnify it or to diminish it. Many men tend to magnify the importance of their acts, diminishing at the same time those of others—a tendency which La Fontaine makes fun of in his fable "La Besace." Yet because of this characteristic, on the individual level imagination plays the capital role, especially in our era, of psychic shock-absorber. And finally it comes about that this multiform faculty may well replace action altogether by a substitution capable of giving an equal pleasure to the individual. This is the theme of a poem by Philippe Soupault titled "Nous allons à l'ouest."

> Etrange voyageur voyageur sans bagages
> je n'ai jamais quitté Paris . . .
> je ne cherche rien
> je suis ici
> je suis assis à la terrasse d'un café
> et je souris de toutes mes dents
> en pensant à tous mes fameux voyages. . . .[26]

> [Strange traveller, traveller without baggage
> I have never left Paris . . .
> I seek nothing
> I am here
> I sit at a sidewalk café
> and I smile from ear to ear
> thinking of all my wonderful travels. . . .]

26. *Westwego* (Paris: Editions de la Librairie Six, 1922).

Yet it is astonishing to observe that this soaring of the imagination seems to correspond to a decline of poetry. Stephen Spender complains of this state of affairs in the most modern countries of the Anglo-Saxon world. "Poetry . . . is rapidly becoming the invalid of the arts, and poets exist now only as a class who press their claims for support on the Welfare State, American Foundations, and whoever else may help them."[27] Must we not find here a painful confirmation of the solemn prophecy that Macaulay made at the beginning of the industrial revolution: "We think that, as civilization advances, poetry almost necessarily declines"?[28] There is, here, first of all a difficult problem of definition, and Gide in one of his last writings insisted that poetry is not definable.[29] But the concept of poetic myth, although it may not be properly speaking a definition, seems indispensable to the point of becoming a veritable criterion of poetry.

In fact, a literary text, perfect as it may be from the technical point of view, cannot truly be poetry unless the author has put his own faith (in the broad sense of the word) into it and the reader will accord it his. It is precisely this spirtual conjunction, called by Jung a state of *"participation mystique,"*[30] that gives rise to myth, which becomes poetic if it is a pole of attraction for active images.[31] A poetic text worthy of the name unites faith—mutual, sentimental, and reasoned confidence—and a formula for activating images which are already in existence. The poetic myth, by a strange paradox, is at once solid and evasive; solid because, thanks to it, we plunge down to the most primitive rituals of

27. "The Present Condition of Poetry," *Penguin Progress, No. 13* (London, 1951), p. 17.

28. Thomas B. Macaulay, "Milton" in *Critical and Historical Essays.*

29. "What do you understand by 'Poetry'? It is difficult to answer, because poetry escapes essentially from any definition whatsoever." André Gide, ed., *Anthologie de la poésie française* (Paris: Gallimard, 1949), p. x.

30. Carl G. Jung, *Modern Man in Search of a Soul* (New York: Harcourt, Brace, 1956).

31. Bachelard, *L'Air et les songes*, p. 38.

humanity, but evasive because it depends on the faith of the reader, a most changeable thing. There is no doubt that certain poetic genres, like the eclogue and the pastoral, are dead simply because no one is willing to believe in them any longer. More generally, every time a poet defers to a fashion, consciously or not, he really has no true faith in his work and cannot create a durable poetic myth. This was the way the school of Préciosité ended. On the other hand, themes evoking almost immutable human sentiments, such as love, jealousy, the sadness of death, and the like, are probably destined to last as long as humanity. It is difficult to conceive that a poet can avoid losing the spontaneity of his feelings and his power of conviction when he depicts something he has not felt himself. This is the source of the failure of that monstrosity of our era, advertising jingles, which are, by the way, merely the legitimate descendant of poems "commanded" or "made to order" that can be found all through history.

Thus the poet must integrate himself completely into the social current which is an indispensable component of the myth. This does not necessarily mean that he must sing its praises. He may, on the contrary, rebel from it or withdraw himself to consider certain representative individuals (for example, Henri Michaux's "Plume"[32]) or special problems. But he will not attain to the poetic myth if he has not "realized" his position. In our time this has a very particular importance because, since the advent of industrial civilization, man has radically changed his perspective. Paul Valéry expresses this transformation with great clarity: "Modern man has placed his greatness outside of himself."[33]

And it is in this way that modern poetry, if it is to exist and flourish, must consider the mythological greatness of a new, exterior world, so rich in possibilities, so susceptible of

32. *Un Certain Plume* (Paris: Gallimard, 1930).
33. "Discours sur Emile Verhaeren" in *Discours* (Paris: Gallimard, p. 149.

an unfolding of extraordinary forces, that Renan could cite Pascal's observation: "No matter how we puff up our conceptions, we can create only atoms in comparison to the reality of things."[34] The majority of today's poets are acutely conscious of the world in which we live, and we propose to concentrate our efforts on these artisans of the great literary fresco of the *"grandeur et misère"* of man in our time. And this is set forth constantly in the idea of force, aroused by the impact which the acquisition of immense power has had on the imagination of modern man.

If Walt Whitman boasted of being "the poet of the locomotive," it is because during his time that machine was the symbol of the greatest, the most dynamic force possible. But is it really poetic? The answer to this question is crucial for the future of poetry. Should we accept the antinomy proposed by Paul Verlaine in the "Prologue des Poèmes Saturniens"?

> Aujourd'hui, l'Action et le Rêve ont brisé
> Le pacte primitif par les siècles usé
> Et plusieurs ont trouvé funeste ce divorce
> De l'harmonie immense et bleue et de la force.[35]

> [Nowadays Action and Dream have broken
> The primitive pact held for centuries
> And many have found this divorce
> Of boundless blue harmony and force—fatal.]

It seems, however, that this fine passage is based on a confusion, because force is far from being incompatible with harmony. The machines which function most harmoniously are often the most powerful. This mechanical energy creates a new scale, artificial certainly, but not in the least discordant with that which is found in the lyricism of nature. Nothing

---

34. Ernest Renan, *L'Avenir de la science.*
35. *Poëmes Saturniens* in *Oeuvres poétiques complètes* (Paris: Gallimard, 1954).

could be more revealing than to oppose the theoretical affirmation of Verlaine with a testimony both concrete and poetic, such as this quatrain of Franz Hellens entitled "Simplicité":

> La machine qui répète
> Le mouvement sans broncher
> Est aussi simple que l'enfant
> Qui répète sa prière.[36]

> [The machine that repeats
> Its movement without faltering
> Is as simple as the child
> Who repeats his prayer.]

Although mechanical force is not fundamentally different from muscular force—a theme of many poetic texts since antiquity—one must recognize that it is more striking and more brutal today than it has ever been. Quite a large number of men refuse to recognize this force because it takes the initiative without waiting for their summons, and this is humiliating. It is nonetheless present, upsetting our imaginary universe, and it must be taken into consideration.

Therefore, in studying the poet and the machine, we do more than choose a series of themes. We put modern literary production back into the most characteristic stream of ideas in our era.

36. *Eclairages* (Paris: Editions des Cahiers Libres, 1926).

2.

Homo Faber and Poetry

THE MACHINE AGE has not fundamentally changed the study of human character. There are many superficial changes, to be sure. Progress has had repercussions on our psychic life; but behind that, the essential nature of the "homo faber" and the "homo sapiens" remains unchanged. The conquest of nature still constitutes the dominant task, and this conquest becomes more efficient as man masters more energy. Here we have our first vicious circle: the more energy man has at his disposal, the more energy he draws out of nature. To this simple fact is due the hallucinating acceleration of progress. Then again, the transformation of raw material into energy or into an industrial product always requires the intervention of fire, one of the four elements, as indispensable to the human race as to the imagination. It seems that we have here the privileged point where "homo sapiens" and "homo faber" meet; fire is a power essential to industry, and it is the most important element in the forming of the imagination. The factory, according to a definition as famous as it is grand, is "the Iron Kingdom where His Majesty Fire reigns."[1] There is much more than a connection; there is a relationship of cause and effect. The curve of the exploitation of fuel resources is in general directly proportional to the curve of a country's industrialization. The necessity of

1. Guy de Maupassant, "Au soleil et la vie errante" in *Oeuvres Complètes IX* (Paris: Librairie de France, 1935), p. 328.

developing and utilizing natural resources results in technical progress which, in turn, augments the productivity of all industry.

In the form of fuel and electricity, fire is as important to us as it was to the fabulous Oulhamr described by J. H. Rosny in his strange novel set one hundred thousand years ago: "All joy dwelled near it. It brought out the savory odor of meats, hardened the spear points, burst hard rocks; the limbs derived comfort and strength from it. . . . It was the Father, the Guardian, the Savior, more ferocious however, more terrible than Mammoths when it escaped from its cage and devoured the trees."[2]   Naturally so versatile an element, whose utility is of such prime importance, had to have a profoundly marked effect on the dialectic of the imagination.   Fire is not only simple combustion or one of the four elements; it constitutes first of all a bit of the sun, symbol of the whole.   For this reason, it plays a large role in primitive religions, a role admirably described in *The Golden Bough*.[3]   Consequently fire, in addition to having great material utility, expresses at one and the same time on the spiritual plane both life ("anima") and intelligence (e.g., Prometheus in Greek mythology, the tongues of flame of the Holy Spirit in Christianity, etc.).

However, modern man, like Vulcan, does not keep his fire pure, and as a result, our world is characterized by *Smoke and Steel*, to adopt the title of Carl Sandburg's volume of poetry.[4]   This industrial inferno and the sort of curse which seems to hover over the workers-with-fire correspond to Vulcan's fall from Olympus.

Nevertheless, the worker is not characterized as "homo faber" because of a transitory activity, but because of the result he produces.   The unknown bard who wrote the

2. *La Guerre du feu* (Paris: Le Club du Livre, 1948), p. 2.
3. Chaps. LXII, "The Fire Festivals of Europe," and LXII, "The Interpretation of Fire Festivals."
4. In *Complete Poems* (New York: Harcourt, Brace, 1950).

eighth-century epic *Beowulf* was aware of this when he systematically utilized the following locutions to name the sword: *fela laf* ("produced or 'left' by files"), *hamere gepruen* ("beaten by hammers"), and *homera lafe* ("produced or 'left' by hammers"). Today the product of the fire's controlled energies is the machine, and this results in a withering repetition likely to brutalize humanity.

To Iron-Founders and Others

Your worship is your furnaces,
Which like old idols, lost obscenes,
Have molten bowels; your vision is
Machines for making more machines.[5]

This introduces us to the third sociological significance of fire, its role as purifier, which gives meaning to all those human sacrifices of which the most famous in literature is the horrifying scene in *Salammbô* in which children are burned to death inside a glowing statue of Moloch.

Fire burns away impurities, and consequently combustible fuel is burdened with the kind of curse recurrent in all extracting industries, and from which the most recent, the oil industry, is not exempt.

Le pétrole comme les cheveux d'Eléonore
Bouillonne au-dessus des continents
Et dans sa noix transparente
A perte de vue il y a des armées qui s'observent.[6]

[Petroleum like Eleonore's hair
Bubbles above continents
And in its transparent shell
As far as the eye can reach, armies are on guard.]

5. Gordon Bottomley, "To Iron Founders and Others" in *Poems of Thirty Years* (London: Constable, 1925).
6. André Breton, "Cours-les toutes" in *Poètes d'aujourd'hui*, Vol. 18 (Paris: Editions Pierre Seghers, n.d.).

But the most spectacular infernal conquest is undoubtedly that of the mine. Geographically, this victory is dearly bought. The coal-bearing regions have cut themselves off from the ancient boundary gods of the country and from the regenerating spiritual power of history. Kenneth Ashley develops these themes in a poem whose title alone is a whole program.

Norman Church: New Coalfield

New corn shone harsh and green, but new brick's
    harsher red
Showed that down there more coal than corn was won.
Tall chimneys flew their smoke as masts fly flags;
Great wheels on headstocks spun, and stopt, and spun
    again.[7]

In France, Dornier replies in corresponding lines:

C'est un noir pays foré de puits, qui fume
Par ses lourds hauts-fourneaux, par ses larges corons,
Ses trains dont les sifflets vrillent de trous la brume
Et cassent le ciel bas que l'air houilleux corrompt.[8]

[It's a black country drilled with coal pits, smoking
From its ponderous blast furnaces, from its big coal
    towns,
Its trains whose whistles puncture the fog
And crack the low sky tainted by coal smoke.]

So sinister an atmosphere must overcloud a wretched and tragic society. The mine-shaft has become Moloch, thus closing the infernal circle. Purification by sacrifice takes place at the level of the fuel itself, without the intervention of fire, and within the mystery of the subterranean struggle.

7. *Up Hill and Down Dale* (London: J. Lane, 1924).
8. Charles Dornier, "Aube sanglante" in *L'Ombre de l'homme* (Paris: Société de Librairie, 1905).

J. P. Fletcher, who was himself a miner, describes the pit-shaft thus:

> The low galleries pressed
> The wide air's freedom to a little thing
> Obscured and soon forgotten. To the breast
> Gaped infants for their birthright hungering
>
> And took the taste of poverty. Son after son
> Gaunt women sacrificed at the dark pit-head
> —It was their devil-god which, late or soon,
> Would have them kneeling by their broken dead.[9]

Further on, in Book XIII of this long poem, the author leads us to the bottom of the gallery. There the theme of the rape of nature is drawn; the miner finds himself at the very heart of the enemy, struggling with the strongest of the four elements, earth, that which—as Bachelard points out—initiates the Reveries of the Will. Reading these lines, do we not recall the Titans, damned by Uranus, howling in the unfathomable gulfs of Tartarus?

> Sweat.
> Sweat.
> Sweat.
> Dust—thick, treacling out
> The roof-scarred heads, down unbelievable faces
> Into blood-circled eyes

He
despairs
> Stench of naked torsos, acrid, human,
> Grease glistening, scribbled with coiling rivulets—
> Of coal-dust sweat
> Smoking the sotted air.
>
> Men curled like vermin gnawing
> At the world's long gut, like animals growling,
> Winning a white loaf from hell-darkness.

9. "Unprofitable Journey?" in *Tally 300* (Aldington, Kent: The Hand and Flowers Press, 1956).

This last tercet especially illustrates the profound sense of malediction. The miner, driven on by greed, reaches the bowels of the earth to plunder. Here are the cardinal sins of theft and rape, as Milton expounded them in *Paradise Lost*:

> Men also, and by his [Mammon's] suggestion taught,
> Ransack'd the Center, and with impious hands
> Rifl'd the bowels of their mother Earth
> For Treasures better hid. . . .[10]

Indeed, the earth, because it is the maternal symbol par excellence, is also taboo.[11] For these reasons, work underground has an immense and monstrous brutalizing power. The man who violates such a great taboo is both subjected and possessed by it. Witness the miners of Verhaeren:

> Le corps rampant, avec la lampe entre vos dents
> Jusqu'à la veine étroite où le charbon branlant
> Cède sous votre effort obscur et solitaire. . . .[12]

> [Your body groveling with the lamp between your
>   teeth,
> Up to the narrow vein where the loose coal
> Yields to your dark and lonely labor. . . .]

And the perfectly sinister atmosphere which Dornier depicts:

> Seul l'echo mat que fait dans l'air la pioche
> Comme un tic-tac d'horloge au loin coupe la nuit,
> Et le labeur plus long se compte sous la roche
> Par l'eau qui coule goutte à goutte au fond du puits.[13]

> [Only the thudding echo the pickaxe makes in the air,
> Like the ticking of a distant clock, breaks the night,

10. Book I, lines 685-8.
11. Frazer, "Not to touch the earth," *op. cit.*, p. 592.
12. Emile Verhaeren, "L'Effort" in *La Multiple splendeur* (Paris: Mercure de France, 1926).
13. Dornier, *op. cit.*

And the long labor beneath the bedrock is measured
By water falling drop by drop to the bottom of the
    pit.]

Here we are plunged into the sinister rivers of the mythological Inferno, from which the ordinary man never returns. This explains too why the poet proposes no solution other than total overwhelming destruction:

La mort allume enfin un soleil dans leurs yeux.[14]

[Death at last kindles a sun in their eyes.]

This is accomplished, as inevitably in reality as in the dialectic of the imagination, by fire. Thus the privileged instant of death appears, that cosmic point from which there is a view over two worlds, one on this side of the grave and one beyond. Fire—like the ceremonial sacred fires lit by primitive tribes[15] which were supposed to help the sun move at the time of the solstice, that is, when the sun appears to come to a stop in its progress north or south—guarantees the eternal progress of the sun on its course beyond time. The sun, principle of life, gives the earth its fecundity, especially if it has been purified by the sacred fire, and thus the miner in the depths of the earth can be seen in a third perspective, as a midwife.

    Hands
    Waiting to dig deep into pregnant earth
    And aid its childbirth. . . .[16]

We know that psychically the notions of birth and death are very close. Death is often envisaged as a return to the mother. The mine is therefore in essence a modern form of the myth of Antaeus, son of Gaea, and of his return to the womb of the earth. Psychically, as in reality, the earth

14. *Ibid.*
15. Frazer, *op. cit.*, p. 641.
16. Julius Lipton, "Hands" in *Poems of Strife* (London: Lawrence & Wishart, 1936).

is a crust covering a sun.   Tristan Tzara rediscovers the
zodiac in the mine:

> Les lampes hypnotisées de la mine de sel
> Font pâlir le crachat dans la bouche vigilante
> Les wagons figés dans le zodiaque
> Un monstre montre son cerveau de terre calcinée. . . .[17]

> [The hypnotized lamps of the salt mine
> Make pale the spittle in the vigilant mouth
> Trucks frozen in the zodiac
> A monster displays his brain of calcined earth. . . .]

which naturally corresponds to the Phlegethon in Hades.

It is remarkable that each of the texts cited above ex-
hibits a measure of disgust, serving as a kind of psychic bridge
between the myths of earth and fire, which are solidly
linked deep in our consciousness.   It is by virtue of this
equivalence that the poet assures the contribution, and even
the complicity, of our reason, which is indispensable to a
complete aesthetic gratification.   Thus the rational implica-
tions are united with the subliminal activity of the mind to
produce the poetic spark.   Beyond this aesthetic conditioning,
of which he is usually unaware, the reader knows—or rather
used to know twenty years ago—that coal is the source of all
mechanical power, that is, of all civilization based on the
efforts of industry.   Thus the circle is closed completely;
the machine age springs from coal and returns under its
domination.   It is Koundalini, the coiled serpent swallowing
its own tail, of ancient Sanskrit.   There is a myth of the
miner because the modern reader knows how much he depends on him, and its symbolic importance is demonstrated
by its extension from the coal miner to a miner extracting any
other material, such as salt, from the earth.   We are
presented with a triangular aesthetic: man, nature, and
industry.   And this is a transposition of that other famous
trinity: man, nature, and war, which can be found, for

17. *Cinéma calendrier du coeur abstrait* (Paris: Au Sans Pareil, 1920).

example, in the legend of the death of Roland taken up by Vigny in "Le Cor." It is analogous to the most primitive of all triangles: father, mother, and child, in the sense that the child results from a sort of fertile fight between the sexes. The industrial effort, moreover, is a struggle which seems to be without solution; man can wrest nature's treasures from her heart only at the risk of his life. On the individual level the struggle is hopeless, but the mere fact that it is continued confers a semblance of epic grandeur upon the origins of mechanical civilization. This rape is not despicable because it is fructifying and full of danger.

In studying the problem of fire, there is another step of the industrial revolution to consider. Thanks to fire, a purifying and dangerous ally, man has attained domination over the world. In the transformation of matter by fire there is a magnificent theme which brings forth violent and ardent poetical sentiments in Verhaeren.

> Et vous enfin, batteurs de fer, forgeurs d'airain,
> Visages d'encre et d'or trouant l'ombre et la brume,
> Dos musculeux tendus ou ramassés, soudain,
> Autour de grands brasiers et d'énormes enclumes, . . .[18]

> [And finally you, hammerers of iron, forgers of brass,
> Faces of ink and gold breaching the shadow and fog,
> Brawny backs stretched or crouched, sudden,
> Around great coal fires and huge anvils, . . .]

And in Victor Hugo:

> Et lui, poussant du pied tout ce métal sonore,
> Il courait à la cuve où bouillonnait encore
>   Le monument promis.
> Le moule en était fait d'une de ses pensées.
> Dans la fournaise ardente il jetait à brassées
>   Les canons ennemis![19]

18. Verhaeren, *op. cit.*
19. "A la colonne" in *Les Chants du crépuscule.*

[And he, kicking aside all that sonorous metal,
Ran to the vat where the promised monument was
    still seething.
Its matrix was made of one of his thoughts.
Into the furnace he flung armfuls of enemy cannons!]

Still, the second text, more fluid than the first, lays the emphasis on the origin rather than on the execution. The mysterious effect remains unchanged, but it is obtained by different means. On the one hand there is color and concrete solidity, and on the other, the fluidity of abstraction. In a description similar to the last, Luc Durtain presents the glass-blowers, and underlines too the aspect of mystery by calling up in us the complex of the Alchemist in dizzying imagery. But the poetry lies entirely in the idea, and it is skillfully worked.

Les halls obscurs où, élevant de fours, soleils carrés,
Leurs boules rouges, les souffleurs, noirs et splendides
    dieux planétaires,
Tournent lentement et s'évitent, puis la canne pru-
    dente entre au moule
L'anse ou la tige soudée, le recuit, muet enfer de
    flammes bleues. . . .[20]

[Somber halls where, lifting from furnaces, square
    suns,
Their glowing balls, the glass-blowers, splendid black
    planetary gods,
Slowly turn and avoid each other; then the careful
    blowing-iron puts into the matrix
The handle or fused stem, bakes it again, mute inferno
    of blue flames. . . .]

We feel ourselves quivering before this evocation as before the mysterious beauty of a primitive painting.

20. "Lise à la verrerie" in *Lise* (Paris: Crès, 1918).

Here the cosmic has entered the factory, but the opposite procedure is possible, and it is curious to see it embody itself in a poem composed on the romantic model which Musset had already parodied in his "Ballade à la lune."

> The Moon's an open furnace door
> Where all can see the blast,
> We shovel in our blackest griefs,
> Upon that grate are cast
>
> Our aching burdens, loves and fears
> And underneath them wait
> Paper and tar and pitch and pine
> Called strife and blood and hate.[21]

This allegory is far from being the inexplicable result of chance. Otto Rank, in his book *The Trauma of Birth*,[22] includes a psychoanalytic study of Egyptian sun-worship which elucidates the meaning of the two stanzas above. The moon (Isis) is the mother, sister, and wife of the sun (Osiris). This relationship explains the metaphor of the furnace door which, superficially, would seem better adapted to the sun than to the moon. The moon, linked to the night, is pre-eminently a symbol of the mother and will later be dethroned by the sun, symbol of the father. This is justified because every night Osiris goes to the kingdom of the dead, and thus satisfies the original desire for union with the mother, a desire which psychically compensates for all our sufferings and rids us of them—exactly as the purifying fire of primitive religions has the power to banish pain. We have here a kind of industrial catharsis through which our age tries to adapt itself to the civilization of the machine. These efforts are still pathetic because the catharsis, as always, is dearly bought. This is Carl Sandburg's description:

21. Vachel Lindsay, "What the Coal-Heaver Said" in *Collected Poems* (New York: Macmillan, 1923).
22. (New York: Harcourt, Brace, 1929).

A bar of steel—it is only
Smoke at the heart of it, smoke and the blood of a
man.
A runner of fire ran in it, ran out, ran somewhere else,
And left—smoke and the blood of a man
And the finished steel, chilled and blue.[23]

Still, if man left nothing but his blood, he would come off cheap. But in the machine age he seems to lose even his intellectual integrity, which he sacrifices on the altar of the new god. He renounces thought, as in Paul Morand's feverish and labored hymn to "Business."

5,000 dollars
à qui prouvera
qu'on peut faire entendre un mot dans l'usine
à l'heure où l'on forge les chaudières tubulaires.
Les châssis s'envolent, suspendus;
le crâne éclate
sur les marteaux-pilons.
J'aime ça.[24]

[$5000
To whoever can prove
That a word can be heard in the factory
When they are forging copper-tube boilers.
The hanging chassis take flight,
The skull bursts upon the power hammers.
I like that.]

We could hardly judge better the decline of human values expressed in the poem than by putting it beside these lines of Boileau:

. . . un affreux serrurier, laborieux Vulcain,
Qu'éveillera bientôt l'ardente soif du gain,
Avec un fer maudit, qu'à grand bruit il apprête,

23. "Smoke and Steel" in *op. cit.*
24. *Feuilles de température* (Paris: Au Sans Pareil, 1920).

De cent coups de marteau me va fendre la tête.²⁵

[. . . a frightful locksmith, a laborious Vulcan,
Whom the burning thirst for profit will soon awaken,
With an accursed iron prepared in a great din,
Will split my head with a hundred hammer-blows.]

There is a greater difference between these two poems than
that which separates the acceptance from the refusal. There
is also manifest a psychical opposition. Boileau aspires after
solitude in order to converse with himself, while the typical
American described by Morand utilizes the rhythm of the
machine to avoid this tête-à-tête which would be unendur-
able to him. It is understandable that a humanist like Jules
Romains should revolt and attack the progressive White
Man, unmasking his inexpiable sin.

Tes forces mal à toi, mechantes filles du feu roux,
Tes forces qu'un fil conduit et que moulinent des
    roues,
Tes forces de dieu voleur dont tu n'as jamais assez!²⁶

[Woe to your baneful powers, wicked daughters of
    red fire,
Your powers conducted by wire and milled by wheels,
Your robber god's powers which are never enough
    for you!]

Erasmus Darwin reveals to us in a curious poem the origin
of this mechanical force, the transformation of caloric energy
into motive power, of fire into movement through the in-
strumentality of steam.

Nymphs! You. . .
Bade round the youth explosive steam aspire,
In gathering clouds, and wing'd the wave with fire;

25. Satire VI.
26. Jules Romains, "Cinquième chant" in L'Homme blanc (Paris:
Flammarion, 1937).

> Bade with cold streams the quick expansion stop,
> And sunk the immense of vapour to a drop.—
> Press'd by the ponderous air the Piston falls
> Resistless, sliding through its iron walls;
> Quick moves the balanced beam, of giant birth,
> Wields its large limbs, and nodding shakes the earth.[27]

But it is to Rudyard Kipling that we really owe the saga of the machine in all its fullness. Unfortunately, it is impossible for us to quote in its entirety the long poem entitled "The Secret of the Machines," which is in itself a complete history of machines from their material and spiritual conception (the stages of mineral extraction and the engineer's plan) up to the moment when, simply nourished on water, coal, and oil, they come to life and move with precision to a thousandth of an inch . . . and immediately become the absolute slave of man, ready to serve him twenty-four hours a day! And what power!

> We can print and plough and weave and heat and
>   light,
> We can run and jump and swim and fly and dive,
> We can see and hear and count and read and write!

This is the marvel: semi-divine man, power, the epic of conquest . . . are we going to lose our heads? We must be very careful not to do so, and Kipling, a moralist like every self-respecting Englishman, draws the following conclusion, which is unfortunately true:

> But remember, please, the Law by which we live,
>   We are not built to comprehend a lie,
> We can neither love nor pity nor forgive.
>   If you make a slip in handling us you die![28]

27. "Canto I, vi" of *Botanic Garden*, quoted by Dr. Francis D. Klingender in *Art and the Industrial Revolution* (London: N. Carrington, 1947), p. 32.
28. *Rudyard Kipling's Verse* (New York: Doubleday, 1944).

Thus the modern age tends to be inhuman, tends to rein-
troduce into our lives that notion of "fatum" which characterized the ancient world, which we find in the Wotan of
Scandanavian mythology, "the god of driving force." One
slip means death. But it is this very idea which provides so
much poetry for mythologies and sagas. It is Laius who,
in spite of the oracle, has a son. It is Athalie who worries
over a dream. It is Clytemnestra taking Aegisthus as her
lover. . . . This perpetual and obscure menace gives a
poetic uncertainty to life at the very moment when the
disparity between the initial fault and the final punishment
excites our pity. This is accentuated when the punishment,
unjust by all human standards, is executed with a cold, mechanical precision. The machine often plays a role analogous
to the wicked giant of the myths. Is it not a sort of Minotaur
which Julius Lipton presents in "Rhythm"?

> Roar on, Machine, roar on, roar on,
>   Drown the workers' moaning;
> Louder, Machine, louder, louder,
>   Drown our feeble groaning.
> Eat, eat, Machine, eat, eat, eat, eat,
>   Our limbs are for your meal. . . .[29]

Thus the poet experiences the tragedy of the industrial
age. In humanity's great effort to snatch its well-being from
nature, human blood must pay the price. If once the
sacrifice of Iphigenia was necessary to drive forth the Greek
fleet, today our ships' engines are built in factories where
workers have been sacrificed, and coal is dug from pits where
miners have died. Perhaps oil and atomic power are yet
more murderous than coal. The machine age has not
exempted man from the tribute he owes to the mysterious
forces of the beyond. There is, however, one notable difference in the present age. If ancient and modern man both

29. Lipton, *op. cit.*

feel themselves to be the playthings of a power beyond themselves, modern man has, in addition, the feeling of having created this power, of being physically capable of ridding himself of it, but of not having the moral strength to do so. We inflict upon ourselves a sort of perpetual punishment from which springs the latent masochism of our age, analogous to that of the flagellant monks of the Middle Ages; but we do not even have any more the prospect of gaining salvation through our sufferings. In this revenge of the material world, the order of which has been upset by the industrial movement, lies a source of irremediable despair.

Consequently many poets turn toward the masses to see how they react, and they interpret the common man according to the tendency of their own psychological make-up. Some, seized by an epico-lyrical fever, exalt the masses. Among these is the bard of the machine age, Verhaeren:

> Groupes de travailleurs, fiévreux et haletants,
> Qui vous dressez et qui passez au long des temps
> Avec le rêve au front des utiles victoires . . .
> Quelles lignes fières de vaillance et de gloire
> Vous inscrivez tragiquement dans ma mémoire![30]

> [Bands of workers, feverish and panting,
> Rising up and passing through time
> With the dream of useful victories on your brows . . .
> What proud lines of courage and glory
> You inscribe tragically in my memory!

Across the Atlantic, Walt Whitman also exults:

> Of Life immense in passion, pulse, and power,
> Cheerful, for freest action form'd under the laws
>   divine,
> The Modern Man I sing.[31]

30. Verhaeren, "L'Effort" in *op. cit.*
31. "One's-Self I Sing" in *Leaves of Grass.*

But always, behind the grandeur of the effort, we have the spectre of inhuman weariness and sordid misery. Another American, Trumbull Stickney, having evoked the shrill call of a siren on a cold evening, shows us a wretched flock of workers returning to their humble dwellings, and continues:

> I love you, human labourers. Good-night!
> Good-night to all the blackened arms that ache![32]

And finally, above everything else, hovers the theme of great tragedy, the mechanical Nemesis indefatigably pursuing man with her greatest threat, that of making him useless. Driven out by the productive machine, the individual ceases to be able to justify his existence. Stephen Spender in England and Carl Sandburg in America have drawn poignant variations upon this theme. We will cite the latter since he develops simultaneously the cause and the result—without, however, being able to explain the connection, which remains mysterious in this mechanical universe, where machines which produce riches also produce poverty through unemployment.

> The man in the street is fed
> Here and there a man in the street
> is young, hard as nails,
> cold with questions he asks
> from his burning insides.
>> Bred in a motorized world of trial and error
>> He measures by millionths of an inch,
>> Knows ball bearings from spiral gearings,
>> Chain transmission, heat treatment of steel,
>> Speeds and feeds of automatic screw machines,
>> Having handled electric tools
>> With pistol grip and trigger switch.
> Yet he can't connect and he can name thousands
> Like himself idle amid plants also idle.[33]

32. "Six O'Clock" in *The Oxford Book of American Verse* (New York: Oxford University Press, 1950).
33. Carl Sandburg, *op. cit.*

Thus through science man has forged his own calamity. Now the greatest imaginable offense is done to him. The technical progress to which he has devoted his life supplants him. The great human effort ends nowhere. Paradise barely glimpsed remains as far off as ever, and knowledge is as maleficent as it was in Adam's time. We may say that from the human point of view the poetry of industrial progress is the saga of a gigantic failure and of the relentlessly growing disparity between the creator and his creation. Man cannot seek to become God with impunity. The more he understands nature and dominates matter, the greater becomes the gap between his knowledge and his moral evolution. Retributive justice, the poetic justice par excellence, is always there, immanent, punishing man's body and his heart for daring too much.

It is most curious to observe that American poets have arrived at a stage where they no longer seem to dare envisage the future, or, wherever any such vision exists, it discloses a return to a blind, termite-like civilization. The French poets are still probably not so much engaged in the mesh of machine age collectivity that they cannot wriggle out in a sort of pirouette, like this by Max Jacob.

Un peu de modernisme en manière de conclusion

Dans la nuit d'encre, la moitié de l'Exposition universelle de 1900, illuminée en diamants, recule de la Seine et se renverse d'un seul bloc parce qu'une tête folle de poète au ciel de l'école mord une étoile de diamants.[34]

[A little modernism by way of concluding

In the inky night, half of the World's Fair of 1900, lighted with diamonds, steps back from the Seine and overturns all of a piece, because the mad head of a

34. *Le Cornet à dés* (Paris: Stock, 1923).

poet in the sky of the school is chewing on a diamond star.]

Among the English, on the other hand, we find the question of the future clearly posed and a painful unanimity of pessimism developing. To John Betjeman it seems that a soulless, insectile collectivity awaits us, as in "The Planester's Vision."

> I have a Vision of the Future, chum,
>   The workers' flats in fields of soya beans
>   Tower up like silver pencils, score on score:
> And Surging Millions hear the Challenge come
>   From microphones in communal canteens
>   "No Right! No Wrong! All's perfect, ever-
>   more."[35]

For Stephen Spender "The Human Situation" is simply, cleanly, mechanically stamped out in six lines.

> This I is one of
> The human machines
> So common on the gray plains—
> Yet being built into flesh
> My single pair of eyes
> Contain the universe they see. . . .[36]

That is the terrible vengeance of things, the punishment of pride for wanting to transform everything into machines. Man has accomplished his process of mechanization but now he cannot stop, and he runs the risk of being mechanized himself. Elsewhere this same poet emphasizes the tragedy of modern man who has a clear apprehension of all that he is capable of, but which he never attains, borne astray by his own intelligence. This torment, recalling the agony of Tantalus, is inflicted on the lucid and sensitive modern thinker.

35. *New Bats in Old Belfries* (London: J. Murray, 1945).
36. *The Still Centre* (London: Faber & Faber, 1939).

... I will confess to you.
At night I'm flooded by a sense of future,
The bursting tide of an unharnessed power
Drowning the contours of the present. . . .
But beyond windows of this waking dream
Facts do their hundred miles an hour
Snorting in circles round the plain;
The bikes and track are real; and yet the riders lose
All sense of place; they're ridden by
Their speed; the men are the machines.[37]

These sorcerer's apprentices have become the slaves of
the forces they have unleashed. Modern poetry is fully
conscious of the upheaval caused by the machine all over the
face of the earth. There are sentimental souls who, confronted by the reality of mass-production in impersonal assembly lines, prefer to look back and celebrate the antiquated
charm of crafts which are passing from the scene. Just as
progress was associated with intelligence, this poetic regression is founded on a simplicity which borders on naïveté.
What calm we find in these lines by Francis Jammes:

Il y a un petit cordonnier naïf et bossu
qui travaille devant de douces vitres vertes.
Le dimanche il se lève et se lave et met sur
lui du linge propre et laisse la fenêtre ouverte.[38]

[There is a simple, little hunchbacked shoemaker
Who works in front of soft green windows.
On Sundays he gets up and washes and puts on
Clean linen and leaves the window open.]

André Salmon writes with equal gentleness (although, as we
shall see later, he finds violent tones to describe Antwerp).

37. "The Uncreating Chaos" in *ibid.*
38. "Il y a un petit cordonnier" in *De l'angélus de l'aube à l'angélus
du soir* (Paris: Mereure de France, 1898).

Le travail est venu chez toi faire une fête,
Les beaux métiers d'autrui sont de jolis métiers,
Le menuisier portait trois planches sur sa tête,
Ainsi que des miroirs endormis par l'été.[39]

[Work is having a holiday at your place,
The trades of others are fine trades,
The carpenter carried three boards on his head,
Like mirrors made drowsy by summer.]

So we see that normally the tranquillity of the artisan's craft, by a kind of osmosis, pervades the town. Since modernism is so eminently a social characteristic, if a few individuals succeed in preserving their personalities, the example must inevitably spread. In Marianne Moore's "The Steeple-Jack" there is more than a mere description. There is a message.

It scarcely could be dangerous to be living
        in a town like this, of simple people
who have a steeple-jack placing danger-signs by the
        church
when he is gilding the solid-
        pointed star, which on a steeple
stands for hope.[40]

But there is another kind of peace, that of devitalization, and another silence, that of "towns which the enemy is ready to surround," to use Montesquieu's fine phrase. The precision of our mechanical civilization has imprisoned man so narrowly that he has lost even his spiritual independence, and for the most part, it has been accomplished so insidiously that he is not even aware of it. W. H. Auden writes a poem entitled "The Unknown Citizen" which he dedicates to identification number JS/07/M/378. The number certainly makes immediate classification possible as it is always based on a code, and it renders human contact superfluous as each

39. "Anvers" in *Les féeries* (Paris: Vers et Prose, 1907).
40. *Collected Poems* (New York: Macmillan, 1951).

of us has with those around him the relationship of a cog wheel to the rest of the machinery.

> He worked in a factory and never got fired,
> But satisfied his employers, Fudge Motors Inc.
> Yet he wasn't a scab or odd in his views,
> For his Union reports that he paid his dues,
> (Our report on his Union shows it was sound) . . .
> Was he free? Was he happy? The question is absurd:
> Had anything been wrong, we certainly should have heard.[41]

The subject here is the dedication engraved on a marble monument erected by the State. T. S. Eliot envisages the drama from the other extremity, at the moment when the young man enters modern society to be slowly crushed by the machine. The pure and simple transcription of the statement of working conditions, such as can be seen every day in the help-wanted sections of the classified advertisements, is heavy with tragedy like a death sentence. With consummate skill the poet allows pathos to emerge from the commonplace:

> What shall I cry?
> Arthur Edward Cyril Parker is appointed telephone operator
> At a salary of one pound ten a week rising by annual increments of five shillings
> To two pounds ten a week; with a bonus of thirty shillings at Christmas
> And one week's leave a year.[42]

In France, Saint-Exupéry lyrically analyzes the psychological cause for this new edition of the myth of the man

41. Auden, *op. cit.*
42. "Coriolan, II" in *The Complete Poems and Plays* (New York: Harcourt, Brace, 1952).

who has lost his soul, so common among primitive peoples: "Old bureaucrat, my comrade, it is not you who are to blame. No one ever helped you to escape. You, like a termite, built your peace by blocking up with cement every chink and cranny through which light might pierce."[43]

Bureaucratic organization is the quintessence of mechanization on the social plane. If we admit, with Freud, that the appearance of the machine in dreams symbolizes the male genital organs, mechanization involves an imaginary suppression of the mother with the punitive retribution of an Electra complex. Thus we are heading for disaster psychically as well as socially. We have a hint of the failure of civilization in the transfer of individual worth to a deification of the community, a kind of supreme and hidden being to whom we are valued only in proportion to our mechanical output. If there is something grandiose in such an apocalyptic vision, it is still possible to stir our feelings by evoking the purely human aspect, by describing this idea of maternity so gravely threatened in its very essence, as does this poem by Louis MacNeice.

Prayer Before Birth

I am not yet born; O fill me
With strength against those who would freeze my
 humanity, would dragoon me into a lethal auto-
 maton, would make me a cog in a machine, a
 thing with one face, a thing, and against all
 those who would dissipate my entirety,
 would blow me like thistledown hither and
 thither or hither and thither like water
 held in the hands would spill me.
Let them not make me a stone and let them not spill
 me.
Otherwise kill me.[44]

43. Antoine de Saint-Exupéry, *Wind, Sand and Stars* (New York: Harcourt, Brace, 1939), p. 23.

44. *Collected Poems: 1925-1948* (London: Faber & Faber, 1951).

We are struck, first of all, by the success of this typographical presentation which fully attains its purpose, conveying the idea of a slow gliding followed by a sudden stop. The text also reveals the aesthetic method employed; on the one hand man, represented by the weakest and most pitiful being imaginable, the unborn child, and on the other, the gigantic forces of the mechanical world which await him, menacing, ready to mold that innocent living material into all their inhuman forms. At the center, as arbiter and an ever-possible refuge, is death. This death soon will be man's only possibility of escape from a mechanical civilization.[45] To die is, in fact, an attribute of life. The body is the only machine which is, so far at least, irreparable.

45. Is not this the significance which ought to be attached to the "gratuitous" suicide (in the Gidean sense) of the surrealist poet Jacques Vaché just after the end of World War I?

3.

The Poetry of the Re-shaping of the Universe

FAR BACK IN THE BEGINNING of the dialectic of the imagination, we have the city. As Bachelard puts it, "The history of the human subconscious cannot be written without using the archetype of the house."[1] But the modern building is no longer drawn to human scale. Confronted by the city, we wonder at the power of our race, and we feel our own littleness. There is, here, a particularly pregnant contrast. In addition, the modern reader, crushed by the indispensable city and all the discontent which it brings with it, feels himself in a state of receptivity because the city is maternal, the crowd which it contains, feminine (*la foule*)[2], and its hostility implies something contrary to nature. Finally, we have the myth of the builder, the privileged character who is able to stop the course of time by creating his dream in stone. The poets of the city vacillate between admiration and fear, particularly in the machine age, and the entire poetical range of our sense of mystical participation plays on these symbolical variations.

This corresponds to the deepest and most permanent tendencies of our minds, as witness the naïve and poetic astonishment of an unknown Saxon bard beholding the ruins

1. Bachelard, *La Terre et les rêveries du repos*, p. 115.
2. See the thesis of G. LeBon in *The Crowd, a Study of the Popular Mind* (New York: The Macmillan Co., 1925).

of a Roman town, probably Bath, conquered in 577 after
the battle of Deorham.

The Ruin

Wondrous is this wall-stone,   broken by Wyrd;
the strong places are cracked—   the work of giants
    crumbles
. . . . while a hundred times
a generation has past   and this wall outlasted
kingdom after kingdom. . . .[3]

Nearly thirteen centuries later, Victor Hugo takes up a
similar theme, man's creative domination of nature, all that
the "personalist" philosopher, Emmanuel Mounier, calls
"the provocations of environment":[4]

Le granit cherche à voir son maître, le rocher
Sent la statue en lui frémir et s'ébaucher,
Le marbre obscur s'émeut dans la nuit infinie
Sous la parenté sombre et sainte du génie.[5]

[The granite strives to see its master, the rock
Feels the statue within quiver and take shape,
The obscure marble is roused in the infinite night
Under the somber and holy kinship of genius.]

Such inspiration is very frequent with modern poets, and we
have an abundance of choices.   Let us take, for example,
some lines from the New York of Fernand Gregh.

Reverie in Central Park

O Ville unique sous le ciel,
Ville faite par un mélange,
Un cocktail inouï d'Eiffel
Et de Michel-Ange! . . .

3. Margaret Williams, *Word-Hoard* (New York: Sheed & Ward,
1940), p. 61.
    4. Emmanuel Mounier, *Traité du caractère* (Paris: Editions du Seuil,
1946), p. 169.
    5. "Les Sept Merveilles du monde" in *La Légende des siècles.*

Quelque chose de grand qui déborde l'espace,
Où le monde s'élève, où l'homme se dépasse,
Où surgit à mi-corps un Dieu nouveau-venu.[6]

> [O City unique under the sky,
> City made by a mixture,
> An unparalleled cocktail of Eiffel
> And Michelangelo! ...
> Something great overflowing space,
> Where the world rises, where man transcends himself,
> Where a newborn god looms up waist-high.]

The continuity of the myth is striking in these three excerpts. Under the words "giant," "genius," and "new God," the poets place the same image, the same dream projection: that which has power to modify the world, the infinite dynamism of the father, which can be found already in the Jewish Cabala. It is interesting to notice the variety of descriptions of this fear which seizes the man who contemplates great things, especially if they attain the proportion of miracles. The Saxon poet marvels naïvely. Hugo, without coming to any conclusion, expounds profusely, utilizing four visual images (*voir, obscur, nuit, sombre*) elaborated by two dynamic expressions (*frémir* and *génie*—the idea of generation). The modern poet modestly returns to primitive simplicity and describes his ignorance (*quelque chose de grand*). A synthesis of these views gives us precisely, in the last line, a phenomenological description of that act of birth which seems now to be widely recognized as haunting us throughout our lives. The struggle between man and nature thus develops into a struggle between life and nothingness, and the poetic development is supported by resonances which reach down into the deepest part of our being. The poet animates things by annexing them; in this sense, the myth of Minerva's birth is re-enacted every day.

6. *La Couronne perdue et retrouvée* (Paris: Flammarion, 1945).

So, inevitably, a sensitive and original mind was bound to resist and place itself on the side of things by imagining their mute suffering through man's violation, and this is the subject of the delicately woven stanza from the "Air de Sémiramis" by Paul Valéry.

> L'intense et sans repos Babylone bruit,
> Toute rumeurs de chars, clairons, chaînes de cruches,
> Et plaintes de la pierre au mortel qui construit.[7]

> [Intense and restless Babylon rumbles,
> All sounds of chariots, bugles, bucket chains,
> And complaints of the stone to the mortal who builds.]

Here, evoked with restraint, is all the pain of birth visualized and not experienced by the viewer, the disgust which is so close to the greatest joy, the depression which necessarily follows the tension of effort, those two poles between which our psychic drama oscillates. Many dreams demonstrate that the dialectic of affective alternance is truly an archetype of the imagination; for instance, one of Frances Wickes' patients describes a dream in which he is presented with three eggs of an extinct prehistoric animal. He gives two to eminent professors and incubates the third for months. Feelings of anxiety and hope. The egg hatches. Feelings of disgust and complete uselessness.[8] The dream process has a tendency to telescope impressions, and often disgust and the feeling of uselessness follow the exaltation of success. This theme is sketched by Valéry (*mortel qui construit*) and by Gregh (*cocktail inouï*). It furnishes a particularly favorable fluid idea of evanescent and dangerous mystery over which many poets linger. This permits the reintroduction of the enigma of the future, which parallels the concept of nothingness derived from the suppression of that which was. All of this is brought together in Jean Pellerin's poem about Paris:

7. *Poésies* (Paris: Gallimard, 1930).
8. Wickes, *op. cit.*, p. 75.

Milliers de maisons, de femmes,
Sarabande d'hommes infâmes,
Tournois de mauvaises raisons!
Le ciné donne Forfaiture.
La marchande, sur sa voiture,
N'a pas plus de quatre saisons.[9]

[Thousands of houses, of women,
Saraband of filthy men,
Tournaments of bad reasons!
The movie plays "Malfeasance"
The fruit-vendor on her wagon
Has no strawberries left.]

The creation of the city has engendered a void. This is both painful and poetic; painful because of the value which disappears, of the feeling of a loss which may be irremediable, and poetic because this imaginary void demands to be filled, since the dynamics of imagination hold it in horror.

This is the essence of the magnificent response to the challenge which Ivan Goll gives in the last lines of his "Printemps de Londres."

Inventons une nouvelle mythologie.
Il faut des yeux de radium
En ce siècle de ciment armé et d'hypocrisie.[10]

[Let's invent a new mythology.
We need radium eyes
In this century of reinforced concrete and hypocrisy.]

This alignment of all our imaginative faculties, this new mythology, is precisely that of the machine age. The decisive test of the power of modern man develops into a double victory over space and time. Swift realization of plans is

9. "La Romance du retour" in *Le Bouquet inutile* (Paris: Gallimard, 1923).
10. *Anthologie de la nouvelle poésie* (Paris: Kra, 1928).

truly the distinctive feature of our feverish age, and of course it is in America that our poets find the most staggering examples. This is accounted for by the technical progress of the United States, but could it not also be an unforeseen illustration of the rule formulated by Racine: "Our respect for heroes grows in proportion as they move away from us . . . for people make hardly any distinction between that which is, so to speak, a thousand years away and that which is a thousand leagues off."[11]   Many European poets were impressed into artistic creation by the American saga. Blaise Cendrars, for example, describes the dizzying erection of "The Mushroom Town."

> Vers la fin de l'année 1911 un groupe de financiers Yankees décide la fondation d'une ville en plein Far-West au pied des Montagnes Rocheuses.

> Un mois ne s'est pas écoulé que la nouvelle cité sans aucune maison est déjà reliée par trois lignes au réseau ferré de l'Union. . . .[12]

> [Toward the end of 1911, a group of Yankee financiers decides to found a city in the Far West at the foot of the Rocky Mountains. Before a month has passed, the new city without a single house is already connected by three lines to the Union Railway System. . . .]

In this unbridled speed we have a new edition of the myth of creation by the Word, by the Spirit, in which the dynamic principle of the father is divine. The spoken word of man here creates things as does the word of God in Genesis. To the solid text in this poem about buildings viewed from a millionaire's office in New York, we may oppose a stanza by Jules Romains on the dangerous and astonishing material con-

11. Preface to *Bajazet*.
12. "La Ville champignon" in *Kodak* (Paris: Stock, 1924).

struction itself with its hint of moist creation, psychically linked to the image of the mother.

> Les murs poussent, blancs, rapides,
> Comme moelle de sureau;
> O substance encore humide!
> Les buildings de trente étages,
> De cinquante, cent, étages,
> Dressent par-dessus notre âge
> Des pylones de bureaux.[13]

> [Walls thrust forth, white, rapid,
> Like the pith of the elder-tree;
> O still moist substance!
> Buildings of thirty stories,
> Of fifty, of one hundred stories,
> Lift above our epoch
> Pylons of offices.]

On the same theme of the astonishing rapidity of modern construction, T. S. Eliot builds a rhythmic hymn to creation, based on the very movement of life, that of breathing, of the "heave . . . ho!" of laborious effort, but accelerated like the work itself.

> In the vacant places
> We will build with new bricks
> There are hands and machines
> And clay for new brick
> And lime for new mortar
> Where the bricks are fallen
> We will build with new stone.[14]

These three excerpts are perfectly complementary on the psychic level. We have had the father, the mother, and, in T. S. Eliot's poem, their syncopated union. These three

13. "Quatrième chant" in L'Homme blanc.
14. "Choruses from 'The Rock'" in The Complete Poems and Plays.

imaginative trains of thought produce a real exaltation, but one which could not endure, in conformity with the general law of tension and depression. That, however, is a good thing, since the essence of poetry resides in the variety of themes and, aesthetically, one cannot remain permanently on a plane of wonder. Moreover, there is something unhealthy about the very rapidity of these prodigious upheavals, which is too reminiscent of the original traumatism to allow us to lull ourselves into a feeling of false security. The individual feels himself threatened in his integrity. He has given too much, and he is not sure what he is going to receive. He suffers from a confusion of symbols, like that of the neurotic woman who dreamed of the Virgin Mary in the pose of the Statue of Liberty,[15] and he runs the risk of becoming inhibited.[16] In describing this anxiety, the poet remains faithful not only to an exact definition of the reality of things, but also to an aesthetic and psychological law; for myth, in order to have a profound effect, must always be more or less menacing. The deepest poetry is hidden in the very uncertainty of the conquest which sustains the reader's interest and thus assures his effective participation. Therefore we will not be surprised to see Cendrars, Romains, and Eliot all take the same direction and attempt to undermine, once and for all, the arrogant feeling of security that might arise from their magnificent descriptions of the constructive effort. "The Mushroom Town," starting with wonder and solidity, peters out and ends on a complex of total intellectual impotence complicated by exhibitionism.

> Par une sorte de superstition on ne sait comment
> baptiser la ville, et un concours est ouvert avec une

15. Wickes, *op. cit.*, p. 109.

16. Sandor Ferenczi, "The Symbolism of the Bridge" in *Further Contributions to the Theory and Technique of Psychoanalysis* (London: The Hogarth Press, 1926), p. 352. Apropos of inhibition, the author affirms that sexual impotence is the typical ailment of the modern age.

tombola et des prix par le plus grand journal qui cherche également un nom.[17]

[Because of a kind of superstition, it is impossible to find a name for the city, and a contest with a lottery and prizes is opened by the largest newspaper which is also looking for a name.]

Jules Romains concludes his poem by insisting on the dangerous nervous tension suffered by the White Man who is unable to support the burden of his work. To this end he selects the metaphor of the bridge, which has a well-determined symbolic meaning for psychoanalysts:[18] the member which unites the two parents, and the link between life and nothingness. In the neurosis of the bridge there is a focusing of the painful anxiety of life and a profound frustration which illuminate, without resolving, the discomfort felt by the reader in the last quatrain.

Là-bas, ton fils, homme blanc,
S'avance en serrant les dents
Sur un pont—un pont tremblant—
Jusqu'au bout de ta pensée.[19]

[Down there, white man, your son
Goes forward, gritting his teeth,
Onto a bridge, a trembling bridge,
Right to the very end of your thought.]

As for Eliot, he leaves the individual and plunges into the social. At the same time, he keeps to the concrete vein of inspiration, finding his theme in the real world, and he shows us the builder defeated by the most abject affliction of our civilization: unemployment, with its blighting sense of uselessness and sterility. This note recurs in a striking manner, with the same rhythm as before, but in a minor key.

17. Cendrars, *op. cit.*
18. Ferenczi, *op. cit.*
19. *L'Homme blanc.*

No man has hired us
With pocketed hands
And lowered faces
We stand about in open places
And shiver in unlit rooms.[20]

To this we could add the long poem by Archibald MacLeish entitled "Empire Builders," which reflects the same disquieting atmosphere perfectly summed up in the last few lines:

You have just beheld the Makers making America:

They screwed her scrawny and gaunt with their seven-year panics:

They bought her back on their mortgages old-whore-cheap:

They fattened their bonds at her breasts till the thin blood ran from them:

Men have forgotten how full clear and deep
The Yellowstone moved on the gravel and grass grew
When the land lay waiting for her Westward people![21]

We find ourselves continually confronted by the theme of the sorcerer's apprentice, and there is something extremely poetic in the voluntary unleashing of forces which, afterwards, cannot be controlled. It is all the more engaging for us since we are personally involved, and the outcome of the struggle has not yet been decided.

We must still note the certainty with which Cendrars, Romains, and Eliot have distinguished the points at which modern man is most seriously threatened: in turn, his intellectual integrity (by the menace of the mob), his nervous equilibrium, and finally his social utility (the inexorable

---

20. "Choruses from 'The Rock'" in *The Complete Poems and Plays*.
21. *Collected Poems, 1917-1952* (Boston: Houghton, Mifflin, 1952).

march of an economy in which the need for manpower is constantly reduced).

But there is also another possible view of the machine age, that of epicurean fatalism, or serene acceptance, which is one of the multiple attitudes which proposed by "le mangeur de mondes," Guillaume Apollinaire. For example, in the famous collection *Alcools*, these lines from "Zone":

> Le matin par trois fois la sirène y gémit
> Une cloche rageuse y aboie vers midi
> Les inscriptions des enseignes et des murailles
> Les plaques les avis à la façon des perroquets criaillent
> J'aime la grâce de cette rue industrielle. . . .[22]

> [Each morning the siren wails there three times,
> A violent bell barks toward noon,
> Inscriptions on sign-boards and walls,
> Plaques, notices, scream like parrots,
> I love the grace of that industrial street. . . .]

Here everything is considered normal, natural. Man's desperate labor has supplanted nature and even replaced it. There reigns a perceptible atmosphere of nostalgia, but also complete calm and obstinate satisfaction before the irremediable. The theme of the modern city implies in itself a transcendence because it is not an entity. It is created essentially to serve some end, either to master material nature, e.g., an industrial city, or to conquer space by serving as a springboard, e.g., a communications center. The poet cannot fail to devote himself to the rude aesthetic of this utilitarian creation, as does Louis Aragon in ecstasy before "Magnitogorsk 1932":

> Le petit cheval n'y comprend rien
> Le paysage est un géant enchaîné avec des clous
> d'usines

22. *Poètes d'aujourd'hui*, Vol. 8.

Le paysage s'est pris les collines dans un filet de
    baraquements
Le paysage a mis des colliers de fumées
Le paysage a plus d'échafaudages qu'un jour d'été
    n'a de mouches
Le paysage est à genoux dans le socialisme
Et l'électricité
étire ses doigts fins du ciel à la poussière. . . .[23]

[The little horse doesn't understand
The landscape is a giant nailed down by factories
The hills of the landscape are caught in a net of huts
The landscape is wearing dog-collars of smoke
The landscape has more scaffolding than a summer
    day has flies.
The landscape is kneeling in socialism
And electricity
stretches its delicate fingers from heaven to the dust]

Like "le petit cheval," Théophile Gautier, the aesthetician
of pure art, could not understand anything about it. His cry
was, "In art . . . everything which is useful is ugly." Let
us try, however, to go beyond Gautier's theoretical affirmation from the Preface to *Mademoiselle de Maupin* and per-
ceive the aesthetic value of Aragon's stanza. We have the
dynamism of the struggle between *l'homme* and *le paysage*
—a concrete but less bourgeois word than *la nature*—and man
himself is absorbed by the myth of socialism. We have a
curious reversal of positions. Mythical man is permanently
crushing a concrete, hence vulgar and trivial, nature which is
accessible to all. This is clearly expressed by the technical
device of suspending the last line of the stanza. Man
crushes and destroys, but this is to assure the triumph of a
human ideal over the fundamental uselessness of the cosmos.
Through these rose-colored glasses the Communist poet

23. *Poètes d'aujourd'hui*, Vol. 2.

Aragon sees poetry in the industrial effort. The imaginative process is rigorously parallel to the idealization which results in the diverse incarnations of the ancient hero. Aragon's socialism is the Herakles of the Greeks. But the majority of poets do not follow him in this prejudiced admiration; they prefer, on the contrary, to follow the broad outline of the apocalyptic vision presented by Verhaeren in his admirable collection called *Les Villes Tentaculaires*, the preface of which ends as follows:

> C'est la ville tentaculaire,
> La pieuvre ardente et l'ossuaire
> Et la carcasse solennelle.

> Et les chemins d'ici s'en vont à l'infini
> Vers elle.[24]

> [That is the tentacular city,
> The glowing octopus and the charnel-house
> And the awful carcass.

> And the roads from here lead innumerably
> Toward it.]

Here we have the most pernicious sort of femininity: the octopus whose tentacles are dream symbols of prime importance, representing the female genitalia. There is, therefore, behind the city, the ancient myth of the terrible and sterile woman, Medusa, one of the three Gorgons. And we understand Verhaeren's vision more profoundly when we recall that Medusa's eyes had the power of transforming anyone who beheld her to stone. By following the myth quite logically, the poet of the industrial city arrives at the following image, which could hardly be clearer:

> Son port est lourd de blocs taillés, où les gorgones
> Dardent les réseaux noirs de vipères mortelles.[25]

24. Emile Verhaeren, *Les Villes tentaculaires* (Paris: Mercure de France, 1904).
25. *Ibid.*, p. 135.

[Her mien is heavy with hewn blocks, where gorgons
Shoot forth black nets of deadly vipers.]

for the snake has a well-known phallic significance. We
have, therefore, the myth of the male-female connection,
followed by death. In this way the modern city continues
the line of all the heroines who suffer Diana's complex—
sanguinary cruelty toward Acteon—that of the woman who,
instead of being a mother, is a destroyer: Delilah, Helen,
Lucretia Borgia, the Arlésienne, etc. It is the theme of
Brunhild, queen of the Celts, who had sworn to wed only
a man stronger than herself, giving rise to the great cruelty
and frustration of the Volsung Saga. All these things have
the attraction of the forbidden fruit, but end by provoking
a disgust of which the sexual obsession of the Medusa's
head is only an extreme example. Inevitably this resolves
into a necrophantic conflict of the first order, especially
fertile in images. Without doubt, the strangest poetic text
which can be cited in this regard is Germain Nouveau's
"Dernier Madrigal" from which we take the following lines:

> Quand je mourrai . . . je veux
> Tout simplement que l'on m'enterre,
> En faisant un trou . . . dans ma Mère,
> C'est le plus ardent de mes voeux.[26]

> [When I die . . . I want
> Quite simply to be buried
> In a hole . . . in my Mother,
> It is my most fervent wish.]

Certainly this is nothing but the result of that progression
in reverse chronological order described by Plato,[27] a theme
taken up by many writers, and very recently employed by

26. "Valentines" in *Oeuvres poétiques*, 2 vols. (Paris: Gallimard,
1953-5).
27. See *Le Mythe du politique*, cited by P. M. Schuhl in *Le Merveilleux,
la pensée, et l'action* (Paris: Flammarion, 1952). See also the same
author's *Machinisme et philosophie* (Paris: Alcan, 1938).

Armand Salacrou in his *Sens Interdit*. And it is not surprising to find Freud emphasizing the importance of regression in dreams,[28] which he explains most often as a normal reaction to the positive flow of sensorial waking time. He adds, in fact, that the ultimate goal of this psychic regression is childhood, not only the individual's childhood, but all humanity's.

Thus we have an intimate connection between two maternal ideas, the woman-mother and the earth-mother. When the idea of the city-mother is added, a psychical conflict of loyalties ensues, a struggle of profound influences which can only be painful to the poet. For that reason the theme of underground transportation, a transposition of city life into the depths of the earth, is supremely tragic. The Paris metro, the London tube, the New York subway have all inspired poems which are uniformly dark. It is not without reason that the journey into Hell always takes place "pendant l'horreur d'une profonde nuit,"[29] that Phèdre on the threshold of her dreadful sin says farewell to the sun,[30] that the sun hides itself when Atreus makes Thyestes drink the blood of his sons, and that Oedipus, wishing to punish himself, plunges into the night of blindness. Modern man has deprived himself of sun and sky and, to crown his misfortune, he seems to be unaware of it and to wallow in a sort of dreary metaphysical unconsciousness with, however, a latent uneasiness in finding himself so nearly like a mole.

> For like a mole I journey in the dark,
>   A-travelling along the underground
> From my Pillar'd Halls and broad Suburban Park,
>   To come the daily dull official round.[31]

28. Sigmund Freud, *The Interpretation of Dreams* (New York: Macmillan, 1933), pp. 491 ff.

29. Racine, *Athalie*, II, v, 116.

30. Racine, *Phèdre*, I, iii.

31. J. Davidson, "Thirty Bob a Week" in Oscar Williams, ed., *A Little Treasury of Modern Poetry* (New York: Charles Scribner's Sons, 1952).

From America comes still another rhythm, more desperate and more mechanical than that of the Londoner. It is in "The Tunnel" of Hart Crane.

> And down beside the turnstile press the coin
> Into the slot. The gongs already rattle.

> And so
> of cities you bespeak
> subways, rivered under streets
> and rivers . . . In the car
> the overtone of motion
> underground, the monotone
> of motion is the sound
> of other faces, also underground—[32]

And it is another American, Ezra Pound, who offers us two lines in a French setting.

In a Station of the Metro

> The apparition of these faces in the crowd;
> Petals on a wet, black bough.[33]

We see that here, with a thrilling discretion, the poet introduces the idea of spring, of the spring which is so terribly lacking in the subterranean world of hurried city-dwellers. As we have already noted in other instances, the European poet, less advanced, has not yet abdicated his critical powers. One needs the art of a Jules Romains to show how this labyrinth, which develops geographically beneath the city, indispensable to the activity of its mechanical life, is still fraught with danger, for nothing about it is simple or natural.

> Je ne puis pas oublier la misère de ce temps.
>
> . . . .
>
> Ciments durcis autour d'une ferraille chevelue,

---

32. *The Bridge* in *The Collected Poems of Hart Crane* (New York: Liveright Publishing Corp., 1933).
33. *The Oxford Book of American Verse.*

Demeures boulonnées, églises faites sur l'enclume,
Rues triples dont la rumeur rebondit sur un tunnel,
A quoi bon![34]

[I cannot forget the misery of that time.

. . . .

Cement hardened around an iron frame,
Dwellings bolted down, churches hammered on an
       anvil,
Three-lane highways whose noises echo in a tunnel,
To what end!]

Thus the metro, cutting man off from Heaven, appears as
the destroyer, either of religious faith:

Christ est ressuscité.
Par la Ceinture et le Métro
Tout Paris débouche à la Porte Maillot.[35]

[Christ is risen.
From the Circle Railway and the subway
All Paris gets off at the Porte Maillot.]

or of the ancient stories of chivalry which charmed our youth,
such as Chateaubriand's *Le dernier des Abencérages*:

Les Dieux s'en vont—s'en vont au trot!
   Jeanne se décourage
Et le dernier Abencérage
Est mort dans le Métro.[36]

[The gods are leaving—leaving in haste!
   Joan of Arc is losing heart
And the last Abencerage
   Died in the subway.]

34. "Ode Génoise" in *Poètes d'aujourd'hui*, Vol. 33.
35. André Spire, "Dimanche de Pâques" in *Le Secret* (Paris: Gallimard, 1919).
36. Jean Pellerin, "Bohême" in *Le Bouquet inutile* (Paris: Gallimard, 1923).

There is a double attitude evident in all of these poets. They accept and they deplore. Mechanical civilization here rejoins the classical Hell too precisely—in Crane we even have the obolus and the subterranean Acheron—for a sensitive man to do anything more than bow down, reserving nevertheless his right to protest. Is not the mythical Hell similar to the human subconscious, and is not this resemblance the cause of our emotion when we read the following stanza by Robert Desnos?

> Il connus-je des couloirs de chair. Quant aux murs ils se liquéfiai-je et le dernier coup de tonnerre fis-je disparaître de la terre tous les tombeaux.[37]

> [It knew-I corridors of flesh. As for the walls, they liquified-I and the last thunder clap made-I disappear from the earth all tombs.]

Many psychologists think that the important things in our lives are determined in our subconscious. After all, it was in Hell that the Fates used to decide the destiny of men. Now we see that the metro is substituted for the archetype of the subterranean journey and symbolizes "Fatum" or Destiny, a notable evidence of the permanence of myths. Film-makers have often utilized this symbolic value, and the outstanding result is no doubt Marcel Carné's *Les Portes de la nuit,* whose title itself is revealing. René Char offers us one of the most thorough exploitations of the theme of metro-destiny in a prose-poem entitled "Madeleine qui veillait." Here we have all the dream characteristics of the obscure forces which determine our lives—the step in the corridor which resounds into infinity, then the unexpected.

> Suddenly a young woman coming from the opposite direction approaches me after having, I believe, re-

37. "A présent" in *Anthologie des poetes de la N.R.F.* (Paris: Gallimard, 1936).

> garded me for a long time. She asks me a question
> which is, to say the least, unexpected: "Would you
> happen to have a sheet of writing-paper, Sir?"

A request which, by the way, remains entirely without explanation, thus giving our reveries a springboard all the more elastic since it is precisely *Entre onze heures et minuit*—to use the title of another film, one of the last by Louis Jouvet, also centered on the subterranean world, the tunnel of the highway to St.-Cloud. (And the dramatic intensity of the final sequences of *The Third Man* in the tunnels of Vienna's sewers is also due to the frequency of the dream of steps resounding in a corridor.) The unknown young woman in Char's poem is named Madeleine, and here is the profound coincidence, the disturbing humor of Destiny:

> During the afternoon I had finished "The Vigil of
> Madeleine," inspired by the painting of George de la
> Tour, whose questioning is so contemporary. This
> poem gave me much trouble. How could I not
> glimpse its verification in this persistent passer-by?

And this mysterious contact ends on a note of classic simplicity.

> Madeleine walks away down into the darkness at the
> foot of the staircase of the subway whose iron gates
> will soon be locked and are already closed.[38]

Thanks to these hallucinating gates, the metro is no longer the site of Destiny, but its very symbol. By an explicable transference, a daring poet like Ivan Goll can close the permanent circle in the dialectic of the imagination—from the psychological state to the thing, then from the thing to the psychological state—in two splendid lines:

> Les métros de mon coeur explosent
> Ciel cuprifère troué de cigares brûlants[39]

38. *Pauvreté et privilège* (Paris: Gallimard, 1955).
39. Ivan Goll, *op. cit.*

[The subways of my heart explode
Cupriferous sky punctured by burning cigars.]

He preserves, nevertheless, the theme of the sky—adapted,
of course, to the modernist vision of the man who had just
painfully conquered one of the most significant portions of
the metropolitan cosmos by plunging back down to the very
origins of myth.

In a work which deserves to be much better known, Dr.
Klingender shows us what disturbing resemblances exist
between an engraving of a tunnel under the Thames by
T. T. Bury in 1835 and an illustration of "The Road
to Hell" which John Martin made in 1824 for Milton's
Paradise Lost.[40] Certainly there is more than coincidence
here. The spontaneous imagination of all these artists and
poets must be referred to the archetype of the maternal earth
which projects itself into the consciousness, to the profound
anxiety of man about the earth from which he springs, like
Adam, and to which he must return. Paul Valéry, in "La
Jeune Parque," plays upon these symbols with remarkable
variation and breadth of imagery:

> Larme . . .
> Tu procèdes de l'âme, orgueil du labyrinthe.
> Tu me portes du coeur cette goutte contrainte,
> Cette distraction de mon suc précieux
> Qui vient sacrifier mes ombres sur mes yeux,
> Tendre libation de l'arrière-pensée!
> D'une grotte de crainte au fond de moi creusée
> Le sel mystérieux suinte muette l'eau.[41]

> [Tear . . .
> You proceed from the soul, pride of the labyrinth.
> You bring me this drop forced from my heart,
> This distillation of my precious juice

40. Klingender, *op. cit.*
41. *Poésies* (Paris: Gallimard, 1942).

Which comes to sacrifice my visions upon my eyes,
Loving libation of secret thoughts!
From a grotto of fear hollowed deep within me
The mysterious salt oozes silent water.]

This text, which draws from the same sources as Goll's "métros de mon coeur," makes precise the close relationship between the labyrinth and the grotto,[42] between Ariadne's thread and Clotho's. In the womb of the earth we find human time. P. M. Schulh, in his remarkable chapter on Ariadne's thread,[43] goes even further and sees in the thread tied to the spindle the symbol of the cosmos itself, tied to the circular movement of the heavens. This, moreover, does not exclude time, but confirms it.

At this stage appears the subterranean river, whose crucial importance has been shown by Bachelard. Milton presents this significant mythical conjunction between the elements of earth, water, and fire:

> . . . four infernal rivers that disgorge
> Into the burning lake their baleful streams; . . .
> Far off from these a slow and silent stream,
> Lethe, the river of oblivion, rolls
> Her watery labyrinth. . . .[44]

We enter here the arcanum of poetic alchemy: the creation of time beginning with the elements, the profound passing from the object to the subject. The underground water is really a composite of hell and sorcery. Certainly it is a sin against the cosmos to bury a pure and innocent stream, especially if, as often happens, it is transformed into a filthy sewer. "The world is a bottomless sewer," says Perdican in Musset's *On ne badine pas avec l'amour*, and perhaps in this profanation of flowing water lies the original sin of the

42. Bachelard, *La Terre et les rêveries du repos.* See chapters on "La Grotte" and "Le Labyrinthe."
43. P. M. Schulh, *op. cit.*
44. *Paradise Lost*, Book II, lines 575 ff.

modern city.   In Duhamel's *Le Désert de Bièvres*,[45] the little river La Bièvres was transformed into a sewer.   Would this be the explanation of its "desert"—the story of the town which seemed to have lost its soul?   From America a similar anxiety appears in the poem of Robert Frost entitled "A Brook in the City."

> The brook was thrown
> Deep in a sewer dungeon under stone
> In fetid darkness still to live and run—
> But I wonder
> If from its being kept forever under
> The thoughts may not have risen that so keep
> This new-built city from both work and sleep.[46]

These two activities constitute the very essence of life.   The underground river, an inhibitory force, seems a symbol of the attraction exerted upon the living by thoughts of annihilation.

Even if the city allows the water to flow in the open air, though under control, there is still a mysterious discord which seems to lead to inevitable sorrow.   Just as the river flowing through the countryside generates light and joyous images:

> Mais le plus bel objet, c'est la Loire sans doute. . .
> Elle répand son cristal
> Avec magnificence;
> Et le jardin de la France
> Méritait un tel canal.[47]

> [But the fairest sight is doubtless the Loire. . .
> It pours forth its crystal

45. Georges Duhamel, *Le Désert de Bièvres* (Paris: Mercure de France, 1937), p. 1.
46. *The Oxford Book of American Verse.*
47. LaFontaine, "Lettre à sa femme" of Sept. 3, 1663.   See also Racine's "La Nymphe de la Seine à la Reine"; Leconte de Lisle, "Juin"; Paul Claudel, "Cantique du Rhône."

Munificently
And the garden of France
Deserved such a canal.]

so it seems suited to melancholy evocations when it flows
across the modern city. Blaise Cendrars, who is not a man to
be moved without cause, has this funereal image:

La Seine est plus noire que gouffre avec ses lourds
chalands qui sont
Longs comme les cercueils des grands rois mérovin-
giens. . . .[48]

[The Seine is blacker than an abyss with its heavy
barges
Long as the coffins of the great Merovingian
kings. . . .]

and London's Thames is no more heartening than the Seine,
as these two lines by George Barker indicate:

What I saw was Sorrow loitering along by
The Thames near the tall bridge by Battersea
Park. . . .[49]

The river, flowing into man's cities that will last a long
while, though not forever, seems to each sensitive observer
to measure the instants of our life which flow by and escape
us irremediably. The river may be seen as the vector or
direct line linking death and sorrow. We are led to reconsider the Heraclitean maxim that no man steps twice into the
same stream,[50] in terms of this poetry in which the flowing
water induces a rich imposition of rhythm, that of life itself.
In Hindu mythology the god Siva makes a river issue from
his hair. Water is the chief symbol of life, a fact which

48. "Hôtel Notre-Dame" in *Poètes d'aujourd'hui*, Vol. 11 (Paris: Editions Pierre Seghers), p. 172.
49. "Battersea Park" in *Lament and Triumph* (London: Faber &
Faber, 1940).
50. Plato, *Cratylus*.

psychoanalysts explain by invoking the uterine waters—that may perhaps be linked with the myths of Osiris, Moses, the birth of Venus, and the story of Leda. The passage from pre-natal to post-natal life can be written in the very move-ment of the river, and this provides the psychic reason for the river's representing both life and fecundity. Certainly the river also brings fertility to the regions it irrigates, as is particularly evident of the Nile (Osiris) and the Ganges (Siva); but if the logic of the rational image is different from that of the dream symbol, this does not prove that the results to which they lead must necessarily differ, or that one explanation excludes the other. The fertilizing river, passing through the modern city, is sheathed in a stone artery and is therefore frustrated in its mission, and thus reason serves to confirm the psychic impression. To this primordial harmony, in which reason counterpoints the imagination, is due the extraordinary beauty of Apollinaire's poem:

> Passent les jours et passent les semaines
>> Ni temps passé
>> Ni les amours reviennent
> Sous le Pont Mirabeau coule la Seine
>>> Vienne la nuit sonne l'heure
>>> Les jours s'en vont je demeure[51]

> [The days pass and the weeks pass
>> Neither past time
>> Nor past loves return
> Under the Mirabeau Bridge flows the Seine
>>> Let the night come, the hour strike
>>> The days drift by, I remain]

Thus the river, symbol of life, becomes in the city of men a symbol of death. And it was inevitable that a revolutionary

51. Guillaume Apollinaire, "Le Pont Mirabeau" from *Alcools* in *Poètes d'aujourd'hui*, Vol. 8.

like André Breton should rebel in a dream where psychic time is, so to speak, raised to the second power ("river" multiplied by "sun-dial tower"):

> A Paris, la tour Saint-Jacques chancelante
> Pareille à un tournesol
> Du front vient quelquefois heurter la Seine et son
> ombre glisse imperceptiblement parmi les
> remorqueurs
> A ce moment sur la pointe des pieds dans mon
> sommeil
> Je me dirige vers la chambre où je suis étendu
> et j'y mets le feu. . .[52]

> [In Paris, the tower of St. Jacques, wavering
> Like a sunflower,
> Occasionally strikes the Seine with its brow and its
> shadow glides imperceptibly among the tug-
> boats.
> At that moment I walk on tiptoe in my sleep
> Toward the room where I am lying
> And set it on fire. . . .]

It is interesting to observe that here again psychic time is borne out by the time of rational chronology—history which turns and totters with the tower, the modern machine which progresses with the tugboat. Nevertheless we have the feeling of recurrence and direction outside the transient individual and ever-changing nature. This is what we could call the tragedy of the city.

Sometimes, in a movement of enthusiasm for the "homo faber," the poet can envisage victory and conceive a romantic transcendence, as when Théophile Gautier exalts the enduring quality of art.

52. "Vigilance" in *Poètes d'aujourd'hui*, Vol. 18.

Le buste
Survit à la cité.[53]

[The bust
Outlives the city.]

But the modern poet is wiser and more pessimistic. He knows that in this fight for survival the individual will be defeated, and that ruined cities will bear lasting witness to the fall of a civilization. In the first two lines of a poem dedicated "To the Stone-Cutters," Robinson Jeffers, with typically American precision, goes right to the heart of the matter.

Stone-cutters fighting time with marble, you fore-defeated
Challengers of oblivion. . . .[54]

Before the industrial era, man did not really feel himself grow old. Primitive man had no real notion of his age. Time flowed imperceptibly; now its continuity is chopped up for us by mechanical devices. Sensitive spirits were always suffering from this at the beginning of the machine age. Gautier makes bitter reflections on "La montre" in *Emaux et camées* and Baudelaire vituperates against "L'Horloge."

Horloge! Dieu sinistre, effrayant, impassible,
Dont le doigt nous menace et nous dit: "Souviens-toi!"[55]

[Clock! Sinister, frightening, impassive god,
Whose threatening finger says to us: "Remember!"]

We are far from the gentle and human resignation which marked the famous lines of Racan, the "Stances à Tircis."

Tircis, il faut penser à faire la retraite:

53. Théophile Gautier, "L'Art" in *Emaux et camées.*
54. *The Oxford Book of American Verse.*
55. *Les Fleurs du Mal.*

La course de nos jours est plus qu'à demi faite.
L'âge insensiblement nous conduit à la mort.[56]

[Tircis, it's time to think of retiring:
Over half our journey is done.
Old age insensibly leads us toward death.]

Even Musset's Fantasio, the romantic hero par excellence, despairs over time's passing, and he chooses to express his feelings through the image of flowing water:

... I long to sit on a parapet, to watch the stream flow by, and to begin counting one, two, three, four, five, six, seven and so on to my dying day.[57]

In this revolt there is still something human which seems to disappear in our century. Time is chopped up by the automatic signals which tirelessly regulate traffic, for example, on the Brooklyn Bridge of Hart Crane.

O harp and altar, of the fury fused,
(How could mere toil align thy choiring strings!)
Terrific threshold of the prophet's pledge,
Prayer of pariah, and the lover's cry,—

Again the traffic lights that skim thy swift
unfractioned idiom, immaculate sigh of stars,
Beading thy path—condense eternity:
And we have seen night lifted in thine arms. . .

O Sleepless as the river under thee. . .[58]

We see how, for the true poet of the machine, the bridge, a symbol of the modern city and its frenetic life, takes precedence over the river which was formerly in the foreground, as, for example, in Apollinaire's poem. In these lines of Crane we have, perfectly expressed, the theme of greatness

56. Honorat de Bueil de Racan, "Stances" in André Gide, ed., *Anthologie de la poésie française* (Paris: Gallimard, 1949).
57. *Fantasio*, Act. I, Scene iii.
58. Crane, *op. cit.*

impossible to keep under control. The finished work sur-
passes man, has a transcendence which crushes the individual.
The harmonious grandeur of the cables of the giant suspen-
sion bridge, a cosmic aeolian harp, whose long vibrations
stretch to infinity, is joined with the eternal vastness of the
estuary and its continual movement.[59] "How small is man
compared to Mont Blanc," noted the ineffable M. Perrichon.[60] In this naïvely admiring remark by the ridicu-
lous bourgeois of Labiche's play there is an undeniable
frustration which is multiplied tenfold today when the poet
must say to himself: "How small is man when compared to
the results of his labors." The Brooklyn Bridge is one of
New York's great arteries, and the life of this city-symbol
of the modern world flows across it with a continuous and
pitiless rhythm. The individual feels himself lifted up,
carried along, annihilated. It is not simply because of the
convenience that there are so many suicides from the Brooklyn Bridge or from bridges generally, or because it is more
romantic or more spectacular.

> Out of some subway scuttle, cell or loft
> A bedlamite speeds to thy parapets,
> Tilting there momently, shrill shirt ballooning,
> A jest falls from the speechless caravan.[61]

The city-dweller has the urge to end it all when he compares
the frenzied rhythm of his life—concretely symbolized by
the stream of vehicles—and the continuous flow of the river,
a veritable Lethe in the Hell of the modern city. One must
forget, escape. Flight is now more than a need; it is a
necessity in this dehumanized environment. Thus human
time in the machine age finds a special symbolic significance
in traffic and the policeman, the modern embodiment of

59. See also this line by Jules Romains from "Europe" in *Poètes d'aujourd'hui*, Vol. 33: "Tower Bridge en deux, dont les moitiés supplient le ciel."

60. Eugène Marin Labiche, *Le Voyage de M. Perrichon.*

61. Crane, *op. cit.*

Tisiphone, who was charged with punishing trespassers in Hell. From England comes this cry of anguish:

> The innumerable heart-beats
> Of the traffic and the streets,
> The impassive architecture
> And the whole colossal structure
>
> But elaborately disguise
> Confusion and the nest of spies:
> Always the policeman stands
> With the baton in his hands.[62]

Such an ode, based on the diastolic-systolic rhythm, shows us the existence of living time in the city, where the beating of the mechanical heart still justifies the expression "artery" (which has come to mean "principal street" in both French and English), as well as the static, infinite time of the buildings. The time of today's man, depicted thus, is imposed upon him from the outside; the individual no longer lives his time independently but receives it cut and dried by the modern social environment. When Jean Guitton produced his magnificent definition, "Time is the site of spiritual growth,"[63] he expressed an evanescent ideal which the truly modern city-dweller can no longer even envisage. And this gives rise to the despair of the poet of the machine which Robert Desnos expressed so well in "Rencontre."

> Passez votre chemin.
> Le soir lève son bâton blanc devant les piétons.
> Cornes des boeufs les soirs d'abondance vous semez
>   l'épouvante sur le boulevard.
> Passez votre chemin.
> C'est la volute lumineuse et contournée de l'heure.
> Lutte pour la mort. L'arbitre compte jusqu'à 70.[64]

62. Charles Madge, "Ode" in *The Father Found* (London: Faber & Faber, 1941).
63. *Justification du temps* (Paris: Presses Universitaires de France, 1941), p. 127.
64. *Poètes d'aujourd'hui*, Vol. 16.

[Go your way.
Evening raises its white baton before the pedestrians.
Horns of oxen on crowded evenings, you spread terror
     on the boulevard.
Go your way.
It is the luminous, twisted scroll of the hour.
Death struggle.   The referee counts to 70.]

In this attempt at semi-automatic writing there is, first of all, the refusal, especially notable in the final metaphor (*lutte pour la mort*).   To have the right to die naturally, with no fixed hour, no arbiter to measure one's death agony —to have at that supreme moment the right to escape from modern time—these are the violent and unsatisfied longings made concrete by the incongruous apparition of nature (*les boeufs*) and history (the antiquated traditional allegory of the horn of plenty).

Thus we see how profound is the interpenetration of the dialectic of the imagination and the human group symbolized by the city.   From this conjunction derives a fecundity so rich in poetry that few authors fail to respond to it in one form or another.   From it a great many themes result, of which, for reasons of limited space, we have been able to study only a brief selection.

4.

The Dynamism of the Conquest of
Terrestrial Space and Its Poetry

ONE OF THE essential characteristics of the machine age has
been the conquest of space. Three centuries ago it took
Madame de Sévigné on the average nine days to go from
Paris to Rochers, including one Sunday,[1] or eight days of
actual travel. Her average speed therefore was about forty
kilometers a day. Her daughter, Madame de Grignan,
averaged five days from Nevers to Lyon, or fifty-five kilometers a day. Since these ladies were in no hurry, it is
reasonable to estimate that to make the same trip by automobile today at a correspondingly leisurely pace, it would
take them an equivalent number of hours. Thus, by and
large, terrestrial space is twenty-four times less resistant to
modern man than to the man of Louis XIV's time. Such
an evolution has not taken place without repercussions on the
psychology of individuals and of peoples. Whatever the
philosophical value of Durkheim's theory about the social
character of space and time,[2] it is certainly true for everyday
life. To an inhabitant of Paris in 1671, lower Brittany
seemed farther away than San Francisco to the modern

---

1. See her letters of February 9 and May 18, 1671, in Madame de
Sévigné, *Lettres*.
2. Reality is "time as it is objectively thought of by everybody in a
single civilization." Emile Durkheim, *The Elementary Forms of the
Religious Life* (New York: Macmillan, 1915), p. 10.

Parisian. Indeed, psychically, space seems essentially proportionate to the time needed to traverse it; and space as a concrete entity is always seen as a restriction in man's world. Here as elsewhere dreams are the ego's protest against the contingencies imposed by the environment. Since in the dialectic of the imagination the large precedes the small, men have begun by the most radical solution, which consists purely and simply in abolishing space. Mythological gods can travel instantly from one place to another, and the wings on Mercury's ankles symbolize the quick step which, at the opportune moment, eliminates the earth where all creatures subjected to the law of gravity go crawling. To accept the existence of terrestrial space meant essentially to chain up one's dreams, and early evocations of speed over the earth are rare. True, there are Achilles and his chariot driven by Automedon, Hippolytus, and the famous runner of Marathon who supposedly covered 240 kilometers in two days, but these do not indicate a great enthusiasm for this type of legend, and such adventures usually end badly. In the same connection it should be noted that the dream value of the winged horse Pegasus is spoiled, so to speak, by its horrible origin, since it sprang from the death of Medusa. The legend of witches who ride broomsticks across space is likewise unpropitious.

Up to the last century terrestrial speed seems to have been symbolized by images of the horse and sometimes dramatized by the theme of the chase. Then the machine age arrived. The locomotive dethroned the horse. Innumerable "westerns" have as their most vivid episode the chase of the train by horsemen. Usually the engineer then drives his locomotive with gestures resembling those of the cowboy on his horse; his goal is, in fact, the same: to gain the greatest possible speed, approaching as nearly as possible the point at which his machine will break down, without however quite touching it. This demands the greatest strain and care.

Inexorably the time came when the horse became a unit of mechanical force and its last victory was, no doubt, its resistance to the proponents of the impersonal metric system, for we still use the term "horse-power." Terrestrial speed had become possible to man. Certainly the revolution provoked by the railroad has been unprecedented and has upset public life in a manner for which no comparison can be found. The train came to be a means of transporting heavy merchandise and crowds of people—a role which the airplane of today still fails to play in spite of the fact that the relation in speed between the plane and the train is analogous to that which existed between the train and transportation based on animal energy.

The speed of movement over the earth was, in fact, the first accomplishment of the industrial effort, and the density of communication routes indicates precisely a country's state of mechanization. There is here a new situation to which the poet has not failed to respond. The conquest of terrestrial space by speed results in complex reveries, some of which are aerial and pleasant, man having extended and multiplied the efficacy of his organs, feeling himself lord of creation— and others earthbound and baleful, the individual feeling that though he "devours" space, he "devours" time as well, and the journey reawakens the disagreeable archetype of our first setting out at birth. Space and speed are susceptible of infinite combinations and the poetry of mechanical transportation over the earth is the most varied on any theme.

Nothing better reveals this imaginative process of contrary emotions than Wordsworth's sonnet titled "Steamboats, Viaducts, and Railways," illustrating in slow motion, so to speak, impulses of inspiration which his successors speed up or telescope. Here are its two tercets:

> In spite of all that beauty may disown
> In your harsh features, Nature doth embrace
> Her lawful offspring in Man's art; and Time,

> Pleased with your triumphs o'er his brother Space,
> Accepts from your bold hands the proffered crown
> Of hope, and smiles on you with cheer sublime.[3]

Aesthetic misgivings, victory over the space-time complex, exaltation of the beautiful unknown—here are the three motifs which we shall rediscover among the poets of dynamism where aesthetic misgivings catalyze the other two and give them value.

First of all, there are those who give us the impressions of the traveler, the creature carried along, who participates directly in the intoxicating conquest of space. A feeling of cheerfulness over the easy victory imposes itself, the perfectly oiled movement of harmonious, mechanical triumph celebrated by Valery Larbaud.

> Prête-moi ton grand bruit, ta grande allure si douce,
> Ton glissement nocturne à travers l'Europe illuminée,
> O train de luxe! . . .[4]

> [Lend me your great noise, your great, soft motion,
> Your nocturnal gliding across illuminated Europe,
> O luxury train! . . .]

And the American poet Carl Sandburg echoes:

> I am riding on a limited express, one of the crack
>   trains of the nation.
> Hurtling across the prairies into blue haze and dark
>   air go fifteen all-steel coaches holding a
>   thousand people.[5]

In this unanimism of the train, which Jules Romains depicts so well in his scene beginning "Quatre, sept, onze express marchaient sur Paris,"[6] there is really a victory of the human group over terrestrial space. It produces a reason-

3. *Itinerary Poems of 1833.*
4. "Ode" in *Poésies de A. O. Barnabooth* (Paris: Gallimard, 1913).
5. "Limited" in *op. cit.*
6. *Le 6 octobre* in *Les Hommes de bonne volonté*, Vol. I (Paris: Flammarion, 1932), p. 186.

able pride which those whose sensibility is not dulled,
children and poets, experience so well. They do not want
to sleep; they like to feel themselves carried along, especially
at dusk or in the night. Then too the timetable is a permanent challenge to the laws of nature. For people whose
lives are directed by artificial conventions, every delay in the
theoretical march appointed by reason is a defeat. No doubt
it is because of this that Tristan Tzara calls one of his col-
lections *Indicateur des chemins de coeur*, whose poem "Accès"
ends with these words:

> après l'éclat des orages criards ruisselle la mort
> c'est le corps décousu d'une panoplie de la terre
> qui s'égrène au collier de nos rêves d'oubli[7]

> [after the burst of squalling storms death streams
>   down
> it is the body torn from a panoply of earth
> which is unstrung from the necklace of our dreams
>   of oblivion]

Death and dreams of oblivion—these are the outcome of
the humiliation which we inflict on the earth which we are
meant to become attached to, not to rush across. The
journey across the earth seems to be tainted by a sort of
impurity or even by a curse. Adam and Eve were the first
travellers after their expulsion from Eden. It is not surprising to see our two poets stiffle their enthusiasm, become
suddenly grave, and plunge into mournful considerations.
Valery Larbaud continues as follows:

> et l'angoissante musique
> Qui bruit le long de tes couloirs de cuir doré,
> Tandis que derrière les portes laquées, aux loquets de
>   cuivre lourd,
> Dorment les millionnaires.[8]

7. *Poètes d'aujourd'hui*, Vol. 32.
8. "Ode" in *op. cit.*

[and the distressing music
Which hums along your gilt-leather corridors,
While behind the lacquered doors with heavy copper
          locks
The millionaires sleep.]

and Sandburg states even more directly:

(All the coaches shall be scrap and rust and all the
men and women laughing in the diners and sleepers
shall pass to ashes.)[9]

The theme of the terrestrial journey is fundamentally
a manifestation of the archetype of Paradise Lost. The
traveler, half-conscious, protected by the warm box of the
car which carries him, passive and sheltered as he was before
birth, has the feeling that he is pursuing a waking dream,
that the true Eden is escaping him. The following verses
by J.-R. Bloch are based on these delicate and subtle sensa-
tions:

Train moelleux et gémissant,
Couloir de glace et de fer
Qui vacille dans le vent
De ce jour d'hiver

Il a tranché les campagnes
Il nous a montré de loin
Les paradis immobiles
Des petites villes.[10]

[Moaning, comfortable train,
Corridor of glass and iron
Shivering in the wind
Of this winter day

It has cut across plains
It has shown us from afar

9. "Limited" in *op. cit.*
10. "Voyage" in *Anthologie des poètes de la N.R.F.*

The motionless paradise
Of little towns.]

This "paradis immobile" which seems always to vanish is
the obsession of our prenatal life.

One of the main channels of the dialectic of the imagination is the return to the mother. It is remarkable to see
Louis MacNeice combine the two manifestations of the pre-
natal archetype—the aquasphere and the journey—in a
magnificent poem titled "Slow Movement," whose first two
stanzas follow:

> Waking, he found himself in a train, andante,
> With wafers of early sunlight blessing the unknown
>   fields
> And yesterday cancelled out, except for yesterday's
>   papers
>   Huddling under the seat.
>
> It is still very early, this is a slow movement;
> The viola-player's hand like a fish in a glass tank
> Rises, remains quivering, darts away
>   To nibble invisible weeds.[11]

If the movement of the return to the mother is reversed,
as often happens in dreams, we have the theme of death, and
this is the reason for the profound anguish of traveler-poets
of the machine age. The train has not eliminated the theme
of the "wandering Jew"; on the contrary, it has precipitated
it. Having committed the crime of lacking confidence in
God, he wanders forever with no destination trying to expiate his crime, but now he travels faster than ever. We
must experience the anguish of this acceleration of the curse
which rises at the very moment when the human race believed, in its pride, it had abolished it. From the English
poet John Middleton Murry comes this hellish description:

11. *Holes in the Sky* (London: Faber & Faber, 1948).

Train Journey

For what cause? To what end?
Into what nameless disaster speeding
Through a twilight cavern of space unheeding
Through vapours of tears, with a numb heart bleed-
    ing,
Torn from what friend?[12]

The train is dematerialized and becomes the blind agent
of despair, destiny on the march, which does not deign to
reply to the anguished questions of its own creator whom
it carries into Hell (we have seen in our study of the metro
that this is the meaning of the "twilight cavern"). So we
should not be surprised to see a cubist poet like Max Jacob
again try to get away with a pirouette, which seems, however,
to peter out:

Invitation au voyage

Les trains! Les trains par les tunnels étreints
Ont fait de ces cabarets roses
Où les tziganes vont leur train
Les tziganes aux valses roses
Des îles chastes de boulingrins.[13]

[Trains! Trains restrained by tunnels
Have made out of pink cabarets
Where tziganes are danced
Tziganes of pink waltzes
Chaste islands of smooth lawns]

It is interesting to observe that here again our common
sense—in the Cartesian acceptance of the term—tends to
seek logical justifications for the archetypes which have
sprung up from the deepest layers of our consciousness.
When a poet who is diametrically opposed to the surrealist

12. J. C. Squire, ed., *Second Selections from Modern Poets* (London:
Secker, 1932).
13. *Le Laboratoire central* (Paris: Au Sans Pareil, 1921).

method wants to compose a modern, logical allegory of the movement of our lives and the problem of the crossing of destinies, a favorite subject of tragedy, he naturally chooses the train:

> Fare forward, travellers! not escaping from the past
> Into different lives, or into any future;
> You are not the same people who left that station
> Or who will arrive at any terminus,
> While the narrowing rails slide together behind
> you; . . .[14]

Corresponding to this passage from "The Dry Salvages" by T. S. Eliot is the "Histoire d'Yvonne" of Roger Allard, whose tone is just as dramatic, although the drama is less evident, as witness these lines:

> Ainsi maint bonheur voyage
> Dans les trains pleins de visages;
> Mais tous les yeux d'ici-bas?
> Pour peu que l'on s'en souvienne
> Sont les aubes de nos peines
> Et ne se renferment pas.[15]

> [Thus much happiness travels
> In trains crowded with faces;
> But all the eyes here below?
> If only one remembers
> They are the dawn of our troubles
> And they never close.]

At the end of this story which the poet has intentionally made trivial and typical, told in a familiar and purposely matter-of-fact tone, the image of eyes in the third and last lines above suddenly calls forth the myth of Cain, that other damned traveler fleeing from himself, as described in the grandiose lines of Victor Hugo:

14. Eliot, "The Dry Salvages" in *Four Quartets.*
15. *Anthologie des poètes de la N.R.F.*

[Il] se remit à fuir sinistre dans l'espace.
Il marcha trente jours, il marcha trente nuits.[16]

[He began to flee again, fatal, through space.
He walked thirty days, he walked thirty nights.]

He too is pursued by eyes which never close. It would seem that the journey evokes a psychic flight from the reality of Destiny. It is disturbing to note that the wheel, symbol of a journey, was used in the Middle Ages to punish certain exceptionally grave crimes such as banditry, as it was used in mythology to punish Ixion, who had offended Zeus by attempting to seduce Hera. On the psychological level, does this not explain why a sensitive woman like Mme. de Staël should say that "travel is one of the saddest pleasures in life. . . . The solitude of isolation without rest or dignity"?

Be that as it may, the railroad station allows us to contemplate and imagine the journey from the outside, and this is the reason that it has become a favorite theme. The imagination tends to soar into space, but it is dragged down by the static weight of the station, and its direction is restricted by the pre-arranged choice of the track. It is no accident that Jean Anouilh situates the essential scenes of his *Eurydice* in a railroad station: "The setting is a station buffet in shadow. Night. A vague gleam from the platforms where only the signal lights shine. Vague jingling of a bell in the distance." (Act III.) There is indeed a profound analogy between Destiny and the infinity of steel rails over which space can be conquered only according to a pre-established plan beyond our control during the movement itself.

The station is, to begin with, the ideal place from which to observe pure movement, which displaces not men but things. This building through which the freight train passes allows the hidden observer to unload the weight of his cares and even his misfortunes upon this movement in order

16. "La Conscience" in *La Légende des siècles*.

to have them carried far away. From England comes this
description of a "Goods Train at Night":

> The station is empty and desolate;
> A sick lamp wanly glows;
> Slowly puffs a goods engine,
> Slow yet alive with great energy;
> Drawing rumbling truck
> After rumbling, rumbling truck; . . .
>
> Effort and hope and love, the heart's desire,
> Leap in the womb of the brain
> As the trucks clang their way through the night.[17]

Somewhat similar is this description by Roger Allard in
"Un Dimanche Limousin":

> En regardant passer un train de marchandises
> Sur le svelte viaduc au rythme cadencé,
> J'ai cru qu'il emportait loin de ma convoitise
> L'inutile trésor par mon âge amassé: . . .
>
> Heureux qui peut rêver à la lueur des gares
> Aux lys de la vapeur couchés sur l'horizon.[18]
>
> [Watching the freight train pass
> Over the slender viaduct with measured rhythm,
> I thought that it was carrying far away from my lust
> The useless treasure heaped up by my age: . . .
>
> Happy is he who can dream under station lights
> Of the steam-lilies lying on the horizon.]

Thus the railroad station has an obvious value for mental
catharsis. One can dream about travelling or drop off into
a daydream of space without fear of being carried away. The
freight train is one of the machine age's answers to man's

17. Kenneth Ashley, *op. cit.*
18. *Anthologie des poètes de la N.R.F.*

fundamental need for a scapegoat,[19] but it has acquired an
element of nightmare horror. Between the two world wars
the famous inscription "40 hommes, 8 chevaux" on all freight
cars of the French railways brought back tragic memories of
the fields of slaughter of World War I, and today there are
the additional memories of mass deportations to Nazi concentration camps. Citing a more independent witness from
the other side of the Atlantic, we have in this "danse
macabre" of the modern world a terrible expiation for the
sins of the machine age.

> Trains lead to ships and ships to death or trains,
> And trains to death or trucks, and trucks to death,
> Or trucks lead to the march, the march to death,
> Or that survival which is all our hope;
>
> And death leads back to trucks and trains and ships.[20]

The rhythm of this poem suggests the hell of the perpetual
vicious circle, a theme which Sartre developed on the philosophical level in *Huis-Clos*. In the railroad station the poet-
metaphysician has a rare opportunity to harmonize his deepest
feelings and his philosophical thought. The union of daydream and logic, when it is successful, can be extremely impressive; and what could evoke recurrence *ad infinitum* better
than railroad tracks extending to the horizon? Edwin Muir
describes "The Wayside Station" as follows:

> Here at the wayside station, as many a morning,
> I watch the smoke torn from the fumy engine
> Crawling across the field in serpent sorrow....
>   . . . The lonely stream
> That rode through darkness leaps the gap of light,

19. Frazer, *op. cit*, p. 579. Chapters LV-LVIII of this work reveal
that the rite of the scapegoat is practised, in diverse forms, by nearly all
primitive societies.

20. Karl Shapiro, "Troop Train" in *The Oxford Book of American
Verse*.

Its voice grown loud, and starts its winding journey
Through the day and time and war and history.[21]

We meet again the theme of time which seems to be a common standard of all poetic thought. The train's hour is mechanical, pitiless, inhuman. Poets laugh at it, but the laugh is a hollow one. Franc-Nohain gives us "La Cantilène des trains qu'on manque":

Ce sont les gares, les lointaines gares,
Où l'on arrive toujours trop tard.[22]

[These are the stations, the distant stations
Where we always arrive too late.]

and in this sad humor Max Jacob sketches the comic uneasiness of "La Saltimbanque en wagon de 3ᵐᵉ classe"—what a falling-off compared with the poetic circus caravan as evoked, for instance, in Apollinaire's poem "Les Saltimbanques"!— which hits on these two evocative lines:

Prends garde garde ô saltimbanque
que le train partant ne te manque.[23]

[Take care take care O circus clown
Not to miss the departing train.]

When it is a matter of catching a train, man ceases to be contemplative, and the station becomes an animated scene of competition between human time and that of the machine. The trinity inherent in our age—man, earth, and machine—is thus met again in the form of disappointed hopes. The station at which one never arrives, from which one never leaves, the opportunities missed, the intense anguish of helplessness, and the Gordian knot of our destinies are all the "Courbes usuelles" which Paul Morand sketches so vividly.

21. *The Narrow Place* (London: Faber & Faber, 1943).
22. André Gide, ed., *Anthologie de la poésie française.*
23. *Poètes d'aujourd'hui*, Vol. 3.

Gare de Kremlin-Bicêtre, noeud de rails,
aiguillage des dièzes sur des cordes de cithare,
fumées chroniques,
décombres de voyages.[24]

[Kremlin-Bicetre station, railway junction,
Shunting of sharps on zither strings,
Chronic coal-fumes,
Rubbish of journeys.]

There is here a sharp picture of deep emotions which we have all experienced.   Therefore it is perfectly logical that the station is located at the intersection of man's two elemental journeys, one of life, the other of death—the great journey. Léon-Paul Fargue, one of the great poets of death, describes the fateful station thus:

Je me tends vers le jour où j'en verrai sortir
Le masque sans regard qui roule à ma reñcontre
Sur le crassier livide où je rampe vers lui,
Quand le convoi des jours qui brule ses décombres
Crachera son repas d'ombres pour d'autres ombres
Dans l'étable de fer où rumine la nuit.[25]

[I strain toward day where I shall see
The faceless mask rolling to meet me
Over the livid slag-heap where I crawl toward it,
When the train of days burning its rubbish
Will spit forth its meal of shadows for other shadows
In the iron stable where night ruminates.]

These lines are certainly logical, but isn't there more to them than the meeting of two metaphors?   The emotion this poetic description arouses resembles the one felt before the famous painting by Claude Monet, "La gare St.-Lazare." Should we attribute such an emotion to the art alone or to

24. *Feuilles de temperature* (Paris: Au Sans Pareil, 1920).
25. "La Gare" in *Sous la lampe* (Paris: Gallimard, 1929).

the techincal skill of the artists, or does this theme of the railroad station have a profound resonance in every modern man? Let us note that the second alternative has, above all, the advantage of explaining the choice of the artist and the attitude of the public.

Psychoanalysts are unanimous in explaining the daydream of departure by the subconscious stratification of the trauma of birth, which leads us to judge the second capital event of our lives, our death, by the same standards as the first, our birth. This would be the psychic explanation of all beliefs in resurrection and metempsychosis. Seen in this light, the theme of the railroad station is merely a form proper to the machine age, concealing an archetype: the Wheel of Fate.

We consider that this interpretation passes from coincidental possibility to the certainty afforded by attendant variations when we examine the poem called "Paysage," whose author, Max Jacob, was extraordinarily apt at grasping the spontaneous quality of dreams. This is the justification of the story that he used to hang a sign on his bedroom door at night reading: "Do not disturb: Poet at work."

> Nuit charbonneuse d'une gare; je cherche la dame qui a une voilette noire sur la lèvre: le bec Auer ne fonctionne pas et la ville est derrière la nuit. Un portefaix valse avec des bagages. Allons-nous vivre près du cresson géant de cette rivière? On serait sous l'eau qu'on verrait des racines de corail blanc sous l'émail de la rivière: les maisons à cette heure sont comme des fumées. O nuit charbonneuse d'une gare.[26]

> [Smoky night in a station; I seek the lady with a little black veil over her lip; the incandescent burner doesn't work and the town is hidden behind the night. A porter waltzes with some luggage. Are we going to live near the giant cress of that stream? Even under

26. *Poètes d'aujourd'hui*, Vol. 3.

water one would see roots of white coral below the
enamel of the river: at this hour the houses are like
smoke. O smoky night in a station.]

Certainly here the underwater image leaves no room for
doubt. The poet is dealing with an inter-uterine experience
which is rising to the surface. To judge the "cresson géant"
and the "racines de corail" one has only to return to
Bachelard's magnificent page on the tree and water: "The
tree is above all a maternal symbol; a strange image of the
germ housed in concentric nests is the *Todtenbaum*. By
placing death in the core of the tree, and the tree in the
depths of the waters, the maternal powers are in some way
doubled. There is a doubling of the experience of this myth
of burial by which, C. G. Jung tells us, 'the dead man is
returned to his mother to be reborn.' "[27] Naturally death
in Max Jacob's evocation is symbolized by "la dame qui a
une voilette noire." For the English poet, Cecil Day Lewis,
life, running between the tunnel (birth) and the terminus
(death) is also a train, but this time an electric train:

> Our wheels whirling with impetus elsewhere
> Generated we run, are ruled by rails.
> Train shall spring from tunnel to terminus. . . .[28]

We meet the same triptych: birth, death, and journey, in
Pierre Reverdy, but in apocalyptic imagery:

> Il a la tête pleine d'or
> Les pieds dilatés dans le sable. . .

> La source de sang qui s'évente
> Quand la blessure au ventre
> Ecoule son trésor aux franges du ruisseau

> Il n'y a pas de cheminée dans le chemin de fer de la
> nuit blanche. . .[29]

27. Bachelard, *L'Eau et les rêves*, p. 99.
28. "As One Who Wanders into Old Workings" in *The Faber Book of Modern Verse* (London: Faber & Faber, 1936).
29. "Il a la tête" in *Poètes d'aujourd'hui*, Vol. 25.

[His head is full of gold
His feet spread in the sand. . .

The fountain of blood that is spoiled
When the wound in its belly
Gushes its treasure to the edge of the stream

There is no smoke-stack on the railroad of the white
    night. . . .]

This metaphor of the immobilized journey is very close to
the railroad station. We have a compact theme whose tension, in this last poem especially, is near the bursting point.
By a very natural psychic compensation, an abandoned station
will be a haven of peace suitable to the sweet reveries of a
lullaby; if its past activity is imagined, the present stillness
will be enhanced. The station is a house or building with a
fault, that is, a human symbol which allows itself to be
carried away by the rhythm of the machine. Abandoned,
it seems to repent, although its repentance does not preclude
the melancholy remembrance of all those who, after an event-
ful life, find their road to Damascus. These are the reasons
that this poem by Valery Larbaud seems to justify the diverse
ideas we have just suggested by emphasizing the difference
between present and past, praising, as it does, qualities which
are no longer of use.

L'ancienne gare de Cahors

Voyageuse! ô cosmopolite! à présent
Desaffectée, rangée, retirée des affaires.
Un peu en retrait de la voie,
Vieille et rose au milieu des miracles du matin,
Avec ta marquise inutile,
Tu étends au soleil des collines ton quai vide. . .[30]

[Traveller! O cosmopolite! at present
Unaffiliated, tidied up, withdrawn from affairs.

30. *Anthologie des poètes de la N.R.F.*

Set back a bit from the track,
Aging and pink in the midst of morning's miracles,
With your useless shelter,
You stretch out your empty platform to the sun on
    the hills.]

Elsewhere this same poet reminds us that inland water-
ways have the same determinism as railroads, for they too
are fixed to the land and immovable. So both may serve as
symbols of destiny on the march. In "Images" he draws
evocative sketches of human lives. One of these images,
that of a fleeting glimpse of two girls in Rotterdam, ends
with these words:

Tandis que les remorqueurs grondaient sur le fleuve
Et que des trains manoeuvraient en sifflant sur les
    ponts de fer.[31]

[While the tugs were rumbling on the river
And whistling trains maneuvered over the iron
    bridges.]

In a canal or navigable river, water naturally takes the
place of steel rails. But the imagination moves more freely,
although the constraint of direction is the same, and Dornier,
for example, assimilates canals to the most sterile despair.

Rien ne se reflète au flot huileux des canaux.[32]

[Nothing is reflected in the oily stream of the canals.]

But in poets less under the influence of reason the water of
the canal generates a fluid succession of images. For instance, Tristan Tzara's poem, whose title "Pélamide" sounds
so poetic, evoking the mysterious name of a kind of sea-
serpent, ends:

l'hôpital devient canal
et le canal devient violon

31. *Ibid.*
32. "Aube Sanglante" in *L'Ombre de l'homme.*

sur le violon il y a un navire
et sur le bâbord la reine est parmi les émigrants pour
    mexico[33]

[the hospital becomes canal
and the canal becomes violin
on the violin there is a ship
and on the port side the queen is among the emigrants
    to Mexico]

Elsewhere, in "L'homme approximatif," we find:

combien d'étranges mathématiques jouent dans ton
    sourire près du feu pavoisé
et de navires sillonnent le souvenir de tes artères
les latitudes de ton corps mordues aux chairs éblouies
sous le dégel de tes fines paroles tombant du coin
    de tes yeux navigables[34]

[How much strange mathematics plays in your smile
    near the flag-bedecked fire
and how many ships plow the memory of your arteries
the latitudes of your body, etched in dazzled flesh
under the thaw of your subtle words falling from the
    corners of your navigable eyes]

It would be ungracious to attempt a clear or classical explanation of these "dada" images. However, it is interesting to observe that in Tzara's kaleidoscope the waterway is similar to the railroad in the imagery of less independent poets, and this should hardly surprise us since water is infinitely more adaptable to the most unusual forms of the imagination.

Although in America the iron tracks are called a "railroad," the road itself is far from having the same facility in generating images. In fact the road, having to choose be-

33. *Poètes d'aujourd'hui*, Vol. 32.
34. *Ibid.*

tween man and the machine, so to speak, chooses to unite itself to man. Doubtless this is because it had been tamed by men and horses for a long time before the advent of the automobile. There is no fundamental difference between the Roman road and the modern highway; railroads, on the contrary, with few exceptions, were "horseless" from the very start. In addition, man knows the road through his very body; that is how he begins, since even in America he learns to walk before he learns to drive. Riding a bicycle is the common experience of machine-age youth—though, with the advent of the motor-bike and motorcycles this experience too may soon be history. The mechanics of pedal cycling are interesting because, contrary to those of driving an automobile and to mechanics generally, they do not come between the individual and space but, on the contrary, transmit space to the cyclist. Jules Romains expresses this felicitously.

> Les pentes étirent,
> Les virages tordent
> La vie élastique
> De leurs quatre corps;
> Elle mollit, ploie,
> Colle sur la voie,
> Ou durcit et broie
> Le néant qui dort.
>
> . . . .
>
> Elle a dans la file
> Des quatres poitrines
> Un temps qui la veut;
> Elle a derrière elle
> Un temps qui la rêve,
> Pareille aux comètes
> Qui traînent leur queue.[35]

35. "Un Etre en marche, I" in *Poètes d'aujourd'hui*, Vol. 33.

[The slopes spread out,
The turnings twist
The elastic life
Of their four bodies;
It softens, bends,
Clings to the road
Or hardens and pounds
Dormant nothingness. . .
In the row of four breasts
Is the time that they seize;
And in back of the file
Is the time that they dream,
Like comets
Which trails their tails.]

And from across the Channel, Louis MacNeice responds:

Freewheeling down the escarpment past the unpassing
    horse
Blazoned in chalk the wind he causes in passing
Cools the sweat of his neck, making him one with
    the sky,
In the heat of the handlebars he grasps the summer
Being a boy and to-day a parenthesis
Between the horizon's brackets. . .[36]

The result is that the road has come to be a living thing[37] for the adult of the present industrial age; thus there cannot be machines on it, but only some sort of mechanical animals. Whereas the locomotive was a *masque sans regard*, a blank mask, the automobile possesses a kind of organic life. In this form the machine is truly man's conquest, doubtless because it obeys him. True, it has a dis-

36. "The Cyclist" in *Holes in the Sky*.
37. Cf. André Chamson, *The Road* (New York: Charles Scribner's Sons, 1929), p. 17: "It started from Saint-André . . . up a gentle slope, like a living being, full of will but calm."

quieting power and speed, but it is pardoned because of its gracefulness.

> Avec le fredonnement des longues automobiles,
> Sur les boulevards bleutés qui fendent les quartiers
>   neufs.[38]

> [With the humming of long automobiles,
> On the bluish boulevards that cleave the new
>   sections of town.]

> L'auto violette du préfet croise l'auto rouge des
>   pompiers,
> Féeriques et souples, fauves et câlines, tigresses comme
>   des étoiles filantes.[39]

> [The violet car of the prefect passes in front of the
>   firemen's red car,
> Fairy-like and lithe, wild and winsome, tigerish like
>   shooting stars.]

But we are making a mistake. By tactics similar to those of the Trojan Horse, this mechanism hidden beneath the appearances of living things enslaves man as surely as those which impose themselves brutally, and perhaps even more thoroughly. It used to be that every woman reminded Tristan of Isolde, Abélard of Eloise, Romeo of Juliet. Every woman reminds the hero in Sandburg's poem of his automobile!

Portrait of a Motorcar

> It's a lean car . . . a long-legged dog of a car . . . a
>   gray-ghost eagle car.
> The feet of it eat the dirt of the road . . . the wings
>   of it eat the hills.

38. Jules Romains, "Les villes" from *L'Homme blanc.*
39. Blaise Cendrars, "Hôtel Notre-Dame" in *Poètes d'aujourd'hui,*
Vol. 11.

Danny the driver dreams of it when he sees women in
red skirts and red sox in his sleep.
It is in Danny's life and runs in the blood of him . . .
a lean gray-ghost car.[40]

Here is a real threat. The automobile is the most notable
example of a machine's ceasing to be purely functional and
assuming a personality which, as has been commonly observed, very often superimposes itself on its owner's. When
Cendrars writes:

Des hommes descendent de leur soixante chevaux
qu'ils étrennent[41]

[Men climb down from their sixty horses that they
are breaking in]

he creates a psychological portrait as intense as that of La
Fontaine's weasel, "La dame au nez pointu,"[42] and the danger
is apparent. If the "pointed nose" is a natural characteristic,
the "sixty horse power" is an acquired one. It is clear that
there are enough faults inherent in man's nature without
his adding those he can derive from possession of a machine.
A whole characterology of the automobile owner could be
written, and many authors have already touched on the
question. We may note among them Octave Mirbeau in
La 628. E.8 and Duhamel in *Scènes de la vie future:* "The
automobile has changed all that. It has done away with
pretense. . . . It has restored the reign of power." The most
disturbing thing we notice is doubtless a schizophrenia which
causes a great many people intoxicated by the automobile to
play unconsciously Stevenson's drama of Dr. Jekyll and Mr.
Hyde, the mysterious drug which transforms a gentleman
into a beast being the feeling of power which comes with the
possession of a car. The spell is so effective that it takes

40. Sandburg, *op. cit.*
41. "Club" in *Kodak.*
42. In "Le Chat, la belette, et le petit lapin."

great will-power to resist the lyricism peculiar to automobile advertising. André Breton's attempt to deflate this sort of thing is quite appealing, but he has no illusions as to the result.

> Une fois surtout une fois
> C'était un catalogue d'automobiles
> Présentant la voiture de la mariée
> Au speaker qui s'étend sur une dizaine de mètres
> Pour la traîne
> La voiture de grand peintre
> Taillée dans un prisme
> La voiture du gouverneur
> Pareille à un oursin dont chaque épine est un lance-
>   flammes. . .[43]

> [One time especially, one time
> There was an automobile catalogue
> Presenting the bride's car
> With a trunk which stretched over ten meters
> For a train
> The car of a great painter
> Cut in a prism
> The governor's car
> Looking like a sea urchin with flame-throwers for
>   spines.]

We observe, however, that the grotesque effect stops short, and the last line inexorably reminds us that the machine age has deprived man of his last recourse against tyranny, that revolution that so stimulated romantic poets. In the modern city, barricades are no longer possible, and the motorized police are on the spot with a speed that precludes not only the hope of over-throwing governments but even of giving them cause for fear. This explains the dull somnolence of Jacques Prévert's worker.

43. "Cours-les toutes" in *Poètes d'aujourd'hui*, Vol. 18.

Il marche dans la rue à moitié endormi
et il prend l'autobus
le service ouvrier
et l'autobus le chauffeur le receveur
et tous les travailleurs à moitié réveillés à moitié
    endormis. . .[44]

[He walks in the street half asleep
And takes the bus
The workman's bus
And the bus the driver the conductor
And all the workers half awake half asleep]

We see that the bus, more intimately connected with the city than the automobile, has lost the personality conferred by the open road.   Inside it has all the sadness of the subway and, instead of diminishing this gloom, the sky accentuates it, as J.-R. Bloch has luminously shown:

Ce grand ciel de crêpe et de soie, là-haut,
Quel ouragan l'arrache d'un morceau
Et le donne pour compagnon, de rue en rue,
A l'autobus furieux qui m'emporte?[45]

[That vast sky of crape and silk up there,
What hurricane tears a piece from it
And makes it companion to the furious bus
Which carries me from street to street?]

The bus, like the subway, can become the symbol of group life leading to death, as in Prévert's famous poem "Le Contrôleur," the most significant lines of which are these:

Allons allons pressons
Pressons sur la gâchette

44. "La paysage changeur" in *Paroles* (Paris: Club Francais du Livre, 1948).

45. "La Ville" in *Anthologie des poètes de la N.R.F.*

Il faut bien que tout le monde vive
Alors tuez-vous un peu. . .[46]

[Come on, come on, push on,
Push on the trigger
Everyone has to live
So kill yourself a little]

In the same way, the automobile in the city seems to lose the
vital potential that made Vachel Lindsay write:

Swiftly the brazen car comes on.
It burns in the East as the sunrise burns.
I see great flashes where the far trail turns.
Its eyes are lamps like the eyes of dragons.
It drinks gasoline from the big red flagons. . . .[47]

and it becomes absorbed into the myth of the city. This is
consistent with reality, for everyone knows that the essential
attributes of the automobile—speed, power, maneuverability
—are lost in the heavy traffic of an urban area. In the dream
world it is normal for the most static image to surround and
annex the movement of the mechanism which penetrates it.
Franz Hellens shows how a taxi becomes absorbed in its
element:

L'orchestre étroit d'un vieux taxi
Fait pour deux rangs de réverbères
Plus de festins que le roulis
Des cent-chevaux millionnaires[48]

[The skimpy orchestra of an old taxi
Furnishes more banquets for two rows of street-lamps
Than the rolling of millionaires' hundred-horse-power
        motor cars.]

46. Prévert, *op. cit.*
47. "The Santa-Fe Trail (A Humoresque)" in *Collected Poems*
(New York: The Macmillan Co., 1923).
48. "Sources" in *Eclairages* (Paris: Les Cahiers Libres, 1926).

whereas Louis MacNeice unites the vehicles within a city in a completely integrated symphony. Before this possessive mother, they are totally stripped of the characteristics which we observed when they were at liberty.

> Smoke from the train-gulf hid by hoardings blunders
>   upward, the brakes of cars
> Pipe as the policeman pivoting round raises his flat
>   hand, bars
> With his figure of a monolith Pharoah the queue of
>   fidgety machines
> (Chromium dogs on the bonnet, faces behind the
>   triplex screens). . . .[49]

Sometimes the car even retains outside the city one of the affective symbols borrowed from it, one which we have found in the majority of poetic themes: time. There is, in fact, a curious pantheism of the automobile which the same author notes in an impressive poem called "Riding in Cars."

> Riding in cars
>   On tilting roads
> We have left behind
>   Our household gods,
> We have left behind
>   The cautious clause,
> The laws of the over-
>   rational mind.
>
> . . . .
>
> Cruising along
>   On the long road
> We do not notice
>   The limping god.
> Swinging between
>   Crutches he comes

49. "Birmingham" in *Poems, 1925-1940* (New York: Random House, 1940).

To an overture
  Of buried drums;
His eyes will turn
  Our hands to stone,
His name is Time,
  He walks alone.[50]

Thus having devoured space, we again meet time, with all the poetic melancholy and even anguish which it implies for human beings. In the last analysis, the car is the perfect example of the result of space divided by time; its speed is the best possible measure of human chronology. Since nature as it inspired the romantics seemed to contain time within it, we should not be surprised to find the machine, whose speed is the measure of time and distance for our age, superseding nature in another of her functions.

50. *Poems: 1925-1940.*

5.

The Dynamism of the Conquest of Fluid Space and Its Poetry

THE HISTORY OF CIVILIZATION demonstrates that it has proved easier to conquer the sea than the land. Accessible coasts and shores of great rivers were peopled much more quickly than the interior of continents. These vast areas remained unknown for a long time, and Swift, in a famous quatrain, shows the elegant manner in which cartographers of his time solved the problem by covering the unknown regions with attractive drawings.

> Geographers in Afric's maps
> With savage creatures filled the gaps,
> And o'er unhabitable downs
> Placed elephants for want of towns.

Is this fact due simply to the lesser physical resistance of water, or could it be rather that man is so constituted that what is distant by land excites his curiosity less than what lies beyond the sea?

> La mer, la mer, toujours recommencée![1]

> [The sea, the sea, forever beginning anew!]

The sea, by virtue of this very quality of perpetual renewal, offers a magnificent field of action to the imagination. There

1. Paul Valéry, "Le Cimetière marin" in *Charmes*.

is no durable beaten track across it measuring a painful progression; time seems indistinguishable from the instant; and
finally, the sea is not barred with impassable forests or
mountains.   Of course there are currents, but one quickly
learns to avoid them or make use of them.   There are also
storms, but they are transitory and exciting, and not considered in the joy of setting out—afterwards, it is too late.
The daring ethnographers who set forth on the *Kon-Tiki*
have proved conclusively that our ancestors were capable of
covering great distances over the ocean.   Man more willingly
takes up the challenge of maritime space than that of land,
no doubt because it allows a greater freedom of movement in
all surface directions.   The less dense the element, the less
resistance it offers.   Thus, the sea is preferred to the earth,
as the air is preferred to the sea.   Moreover, swimming and
flying are similar actions.   The sailboat often evokes bird
metaphors.   The fish propels itself through water by means
of a *fin*, a word derived from the Anglo-Saxon *finn*, which
is related to the French *penne*, meaning "quill" or "feather."
And in addition to all this, the sea offers a rest for the human
psyche by taking man out of the element in which he is
accustomed to operate.

Before the machine age, whenever man went sailing, the
activity seemed to produce a kind of synthesis of aerial and
aquatic maneuvers.   This never failed to provoke the pleasure inherent in the economy of a double victory.   The harmonious, organized effort of a ship's crew unfurling sail
creates a feeling of spaciousness and joy as expressed, for
example, in these lines from the early fourteenth century by
Robert Mannyng of Brunne.

> The wynd blew wel, ther schipe gon fleye,
> & the mariners that weren sleye,
> Ilkon dide ther maistrie:
> Somme aforced the wyndas,
> Somme the loof, some the bytas;

The mayster mariner was byhynde,
The ship to stere by the wynde. . . .[2]

This is a proper sort of effort, conforming to nature and not directed against it. It is, in a word, an aerial effort.

One of the first consequences of Fulton's invention was the dissociation of navigation from flight, and the breaking of a tie which had existed from the time of Icarus. Wind was no longer a vital help; it became a hindrance. Sea travel gained great speed. Whereas it took about two and a half months to cross the Atlantic at the beginning of the nineteenth century, fifty years later, in 1860, the iron-hulled steamship *Great Eastern*, 210 meters long, equipped with sails, paddle-wheel, and a screw propellor, made the same voyage in eleven days, or one-seventh the time. Since then the crossing has lost the tang of real adventure, and man's reaction has been to create imaginary adventure to replace it. The less inspiring reality is, the more imagination embellishes it. This is why children often amuse themselves more with a rag or a spool than with an elaborate toy. We shall see that transatlantic liners are charged with incomparable poetic value. By a strange coincidence it was at the very moment— the end of the nineteenth century—when man definitely re-nounced the idea of flight over water by eliminating the auxiliary sails on steamships, that he undertook the victorious conquest of the air, thus allowing his imagination to develop in the direction of pure aerial daydreams.

The conquest of sea or air imposes certain characteristics on man. Whereas the mind tends to follow a firm, Cartesian, mathematical or geometrical line when reflecting on things of the earth, when it muses on those of the sea or the air, it has a tendency to wander, to welcome the unexpected. Humor, a liquid word, is characteristic of sailors, whether they be ancient Greeks or Anglo-Saxons. The true sailor is a perfect

2. *Chronicles*, lines 12084-12090.

humorist, as Loÿs Masson reveals in a fine poem which begins:

> Satan le mégisser fit pour les panneaux de la cale
> de petits mauves de cuir avec un coeur d'épingle
> l'on arrima deux cents barils de vin et cent d'absinthe
> pour les cyclones assoiffés compagnons et du gin
> doux pour les petits alizés frêles comme des femmes
> qui viennent prendre les quarts d'étain des mains des
> matelots
> et puis s'essuient la bouche au plumage d'un pétrel.[3]

> [Satan the tawer cut little mauve leather pieces for the panels of the hold with a heart-shaped pin. Two hundred barrels of wine and one hundred of absinthe were stowed away for the thirsty companionable hurricanes and mild gin for the little trade winds, frail as women, which take tin mugs from sailors' hands and then wipe their mouths on a petrel's feathers.]

In the third and sixth line of this passage we arrive at the summit of the amusing and mischievous unexpected, which is the characteristic reaction of telescoping humor, the contrast between hard reality (*baril, quart*) and the vagueness of dreams (*cyclones assoiffés, alizés, femmes*), which is so full of meaning and so inexplicable in terms of pure logic.[4]

A similar contrast between the sea and the mainland, with the interrelationship needed to stir the imagination, is found in the theme of the harbor. This conjunction produces what may well be called a new human environment. Bachelard demonstrates, with a thoroughness leaving no room for doubt, that the sea is a maternal symbol; since the city is also such a symbol, the result is a superposition that is full of significance.

3. "Le grand yacht Despair" cited in L.-G. Gros, *Poètes contemporains* (Marseilles: Cahiers du Sud, 1944).

4. Paul Ginestier, "La Logique de l'Humour" and "Aspect sociologique de l'Humour" in *Revue d'Esthétique*, II, 1, and III, 3, 4; and Max Eastman, *Enjoyment of Laughter* (New York: Simon & Shuster, 1952).

Pierre MacOrlan, in a prose poem titled "Hambourg ou l'introduction sentimentale à la vie des ports," tells us:

> La rose des ports européens dresse à chacune de ses quatre pointes essentielles quatre villes dont les docks reçoivent des hommages marins d'une inspiration assez différente. Au Nord il y a Hambourg et ses paquebots géants à travers la pluie; à l'est, Londres manipule les serrures de ses entrepôts qui sentent le rhum et le poivre; au Sud, il y a la chanson legère de Marseille et les rois mages à l'entrée de la rue Bouterie; à l'Ouest Constantinople tend un décor nouveau pour les embûches de la Corne d'Or.
>
> Tout jeune homme devrait connaître ces quatre villes afin de mêler en elles quatres vérités incomparables pour en composer une vérité unique qui peut bien servir trente années, la durée normale d'une vie humaine dans sa période d'activité.[5]

> [At the four points of the compass of European harbors are set four cities whose quais receive nautical homages of very differing inspirations. To the north lies Hamburg and its giant steamships through the rain; to the east London handles the locks of its warehouses smelling of rum and pepper; to the south is the gay chanty of Marseilles and the Magi at the entrance to the rue Bouterie; to the west Constantinople spreads a new setting for the snares of the Golden Horn.
>
> Every young man ought to know these four cities in order to blend in them four incomparable truths, composing a single truth which could well last thirty years, the normal span of activity of a human life.]

Thus the harbor is a kind of super-city. It is the springboard from which those who leave to conquer maritime

5. *Villes* (Paris: Gallimard, 1929).

space set forth. It is the haven to which they return with the spoils of useful victories. Finally it is the place where sea-farers and land-dwellers mingle. These are the aspects of the harbor which excite and instruct men and which Mac-Orlan praises. But at the other extreme, there is its passive character of the worst sort. The harbor is situated between the past and the future and has none of the dynamism of the instant. It represents, for certain poets, all the devitalizing inertia of a prison.

> Comme les grands oiseaux prisonniers au jardin,
> Dans le port sans amour les steamers se balancent,
> Leurs mâts font sur la mer flamber des fers de lances
> Et leurs poumons ouverts marquent l'azur marin. . .[6]

> [Like great birds imprisoned in a garden
> The steamers ride in the loveless harbor,
> Their masts make spearheads blaze on the sea,
> And their open lungs mark the marine blue. . . .]

Add to this the calm of night, and the result is a perfect representation of cosmic death, the kind reflected in the Tartarus of mythology, into which flow the four infernal rivers. It is a picture that comes instantly to mind when one reads such lines as these from "Harbour Ferry" by Roy Fuller.

> To-night the moon has risen
> Over a quiet harbour,
> Through twisted iron and labour,
> Lighting the half-drowned ships.
> Oh surely the fatal chasm
> Is closer, the furious steps
> Swifter? The silver drips

> From the angle of the wake:
> The moon is flooding the faces. . . .[7]

6. André Salmon, "Anvers" in *Poètes d'aujourd'hui*, Vol. 53.
7. *The Middle of a War* (London: The Hogarth Press, 1942).

The harbor is mournful at the hour when all activity ceases, and there is no hiding the fact that it is the ocean's resting-place, a concept which need not be greatly extended to arrive at that of the cemetery. However, whereas Roy Fuller dwelled more particularly on the appearance of harbors, the imprisoned water, Jean Pellerin observes rather the human group which organizes departures and welcomes arrivals, but still does not go anywhere itself. In the following quatrain we have all the sorrow of a sterile society, a nostalgia symbolized by a newspaper title flung into the desert, a title which is itself a sign of contemplation devoid of action—the substitution of reading the sports page for the effective practice of physical exercise.

> Je peindrai l'eau, le ciel, le port
>   Et le désert "immense"
> A l'heure grise où l'on commence
>   A crier *Paris-Sport*.[8]

> [I shall paint the water, sky, harbor
>   And the "immense" desert
> At the gray hour when they begin
>   To cry "Paris-Sport."]

But no doubt it is unfair to observe the harbor strictly from the point of view of a land-dweller, making a sort of hybrid of the sea and the town, for in the imagination as in nature, hybrids tend to be sterile. It would be better to generalize the remark of Cendrars: "Marseilles belongs to him who comes from the open sea,"[9] and apply it to all harbors. Then we become aware of a City of ships, and this changes everything. The harbor gives reality to the ships. It becomes the center of a gigantic web woven throughout the world by all the vessels whose home port it is. It is no longer sterile and unloving. It becomes instead an Egeria,

---

8. "Quotidiennes" in *Le Bouquet inutile* (Paris: Gallimard, 1923).
9. *L'Homme foudroyé* (Paris: Denoël), p. 54.

the water nymph symbol of fertility particularly useful as
a help in difficult childbirths.[10]   Then we discover the true
meaning of the advice given above by MacOrlan, for Egeria
was also the nymph who counseled the legendary king Numa
Pompilius, one of the founders of Rome.   Having set out
from the city, we return to find it more beautiful and larger
than ever; and on this magnifying principle Walt Whitman
builds a remarkable poem which begins:

> City of ships!
> (O the black ships!   O the fierce ships!
> O the beautiful sharp-bow'd steam-ships and sail-
>   ships!)
> City of the world! (for all races are here,
> All the lands of the earth make contributions
>   here;) . . .[11]

Admiration, especially when it is as lyrical as this, is very
close to love. Brauquier takes this next step when he shows
us in the harbor the image of the city-as-mistress merged
with that of the city-as-nurse.   This provokes a sort of spiritual incest, which is fruitful for the imagination, because it is
the common ground of two patterns of imagery and, from the
psychic point of view, this is inspiring.   We recall that the
oracles unanimously interpreted Caesar's dream of incest
with his mother as a favorable omen, betokening his conquest of the universe.   Here are some lines taken from
"Port-Saïd," from a collection called *Eau douce pour navires*
(the cosmogony of water!):

> Des villes font ce qu'elles peuvent
> Pour retenir, pour arreter;
> Des villes ont des charmes lâches,
> Des villes sont des lits d'amour.
>
>   .   .   .   .

10. Frazer, *op. cit.*, p. 8.
11. "City of Ships" in *Leaves of Grass*

Dis, combien en expédies-tu, chaque jour,
Pour la douceur des statistiques maritimes,
Après les avoir nourris de charbon, abreuvés de
    mazout, ô Port-Saïd,
Et ravitaillés d'eau douce et de vivres?[12]

[Towns do what they can
To detain, to delay;
Towns have soft charms,
Towns are beds of love.

.   .   .   .

Say, how many do you send forth each day
For the pleasure of maritime statistics
After having fed them with coal, quenched them with
    fuel oil, O Port Said,
And provisioned them with fresh water and supplies?]

This reminds us that the modern harbor also has a third
significance. It is an industrial site which the floating factories, which are today's ships, swarm around. In the harbor,
steamships lose the gracefulness which they had in motion.
Alongside them there are other machines which serve them.
More than ever, the trilogy, water, earth, and machine,
seems to exclude man. The modern harbor is no longer a
poetic point of departure. It has become as commonplace
as a service station, but commonplace in a manner so complex
that it seems impossible for it to be set in order on a human
scale. The ship is the largest creation which man has been
able to put in motion, and it provokes the disgust we feel for
all things gigantic. A transatlantic liner in the middle of the
ocean is in surroundings made to its scale, but in port it gives
an impression of overwhelming hugeness. It is a floating city
within a city of stone. It reproduces for us the myth of the
Norse giant who had no heart in its body because he kept it

12. Louis Brauquier, "Port-Said" in *Eau douce pour navires* (Paris:
Gallimard, 1926).

somewhere else, hidden in a safe place.[13] The soul of the ship is diffused over the sea. It never enters the harbor. The result is a feeling of disgust. The observer asks himself, what are the seminal reasons, to adopt the phrase of Plotinus, which have led humanity to produce this soulless giant, around whom all activity seems to evoke spider imagery, as in this description by Luc Durtain:

> Des mâts, des mâts, des mâts, des mâts,
> Et puis cordages, cordages, cordages.
>
> . . . .
>
> Des tôles, des barres, des ronds, des angles.
> Ça se pousse, ça se débrouille, ça se pénètre.
> Toutes les choses se crachent dans la bouche.[14]

> [Masts, masts, masts, masts,
> And then cordage, cordage, cordage.
>
> . . . .
>
> Sheet metal, rods, rounds and angles.
> Pushing, shifting, penetrating.
> All things spit in each others' mouths.]

This changes whenever fog—a kind of vaporized ocean—invades the town. Then there is no longer the problem of immobility. It becomes necessary to navigate even within the harbor. Blaise Cendrars ends his description of Vancouver with these lines:

> Se guidant dans le brouillard sur les appels d'une
>   sirène
> On se cogne contre la masse sombre du navire et par
>   la hanche tribord
> Grimpent les chiens samoyèdes
> Filasses dans le gris-blanc-jaune
> Comme si l'on chargeait du brouillard.[15]

---

13. Frazer, *op. cit.*, p. 668.
14. "Un port" in *Le Retour des hommes* (Paris: Gallimard, 1920).
15. "Vancouver" in *Kodak*.

[Steering in the fog by the sounds of a siren
We strike the dark mass of the ship and on the star-
     board quarter
The Samoyed dogs climb on,
Tow-like in the grey-white-yellow,
As if they were taking fog aboard.]

Hart Crane shows us, in an original form, that this synthesis of two elements leads everywhere and goes nowhere,
introducing the theme of profound consciousness which we
shall meet again soon.

The Harbor Dawn

Insistently through sleep—a tide of voices—
They meet you listening midway in your dream,
The long, tired sounds, fog-insulated noises:
Gongs in white surplices, beshrouded wails,
Far strum of fog horns . . . signals dispersed in
     veils.
And then a truck will lumber past the wharves
As winch engines begin throbbing on some
     deck; . . .[16]

This is an advantageous line of inspiration because fog
cuts man off from the exterior world and plunges him into
a new element where he can continue to live, but deprived
of sight and hearing, so that there arises within him a feeling of powerlessness and of courting danger. Profound
imaginations plunge most deeply into the veil of fog, and a
menacing deformation is the result. Fog is the favorite
haunt of ghosts, e.g., Hamlet. T. S. Eliot has observed that
a bell in fog measures time not for the living, but for the
dead.

And under the oppression of the silent fog
The tolling bell
Measures time not our time. . .[17]

16. Crane, *op. cit.*
17. "The Dry Salvages" in *Four Quartets*.

And certainly the experience of sailing in a fog-bank amounts to that of being on a phantom ship. Robinson Jeffers sketches a modernization of the famous fog scene in Pierre Loti's *Pêcheur d'Islande* in his "Boats in a Fog."

> A sudden fog-drift muffled the ocean,
> A throbbing of engines moved in it,
> At length, a stone's throw out, between the rocks and
>   the vapor,
> One by one moved shadows
> Out of the mystery, shadows, fishing-boats, trailing
>   each other
> Following the cliffs for guidance,
> Holding a difficult path between the peril of the
>   sea-fog
> And the foam on the shore granite. . . .[18]

Here the struggle is uneven. The ships have to fight against a coalition of three elements, earth, water, and air, and their tendency is to group together, like sisters in danger. This produces a considerable pathos. Since fog is watery, it cuts the ship off from air, its proper element. Thus isolated, the vessel becomes a metaphysical entity, a kind of great living body whose soul is the pilot, which must be steered, like our own body, through the difficulties of existence. On this foundation Walt Whitman constructed the following scene:

> Aboard at a ship's helm
> A young steersman steering with care.
>
> Through fog on a sea-coast dolefully ringing,
> An ocean-bell—O a warning bell, rock'd by the
>   waves. . .
>
> But O the ship, the immortal ship! O ship aboard
>   the ship!

18. *The Oxford Book of American Verse.*

Ship of the body, ship of the soul, voyaging, voyaging,
    voyaging.[19]

But in the years that have elapsed since then, radar has conquered the fog, and another danger has taken its place: war.
Here again ships huddle together in the face of danger like
a threatened flock. In his poem "Convoy" Louis MacNeice
pays them tribute.

> Together, keeping in line, slow as if hypnotised
> Across the blackboard sea in sombre echelon
> The food-ships draw their wakes. No Euclid could
>   have devised
> Neater means to a more essential end—[20]

This slowness is characteristic of the toilers of the sea,
which slowly plow their useful furrow. There are, in fact,
two types of ships, the glittering aristocrats and the other
sort. The former are subjects for poetry *de luxe,* and the
sea as well as their cargo must keep within the same tone.
The others, the humble proletariat of the ocean, content
themselves with their daily tasks in difficult and unattractive
conditions. It is the dramatic opposition of the great lord
and the humble worker which emerges from these two an-
ithetical stanzas by John Masefield:

> Stately Spanish galleon coming from the Isthmus,
> Dipping through the Tropics by the palm-green
>   shores
> With a cargo of diamonds,
> Emeralds, amethysts,
> Topazes, and cinnamon, and gold moidores.
>
> Dirty British coaster with a salt-caked smoke stack,
> Butting through the Channel in the mad March days
> With a cargo of Tyne coal,

19. "Aboard at a Ship's Helm" in *Leaves of Grass.*
20. *Springboard* (London: Faber & Faber, 1944).

Road rails, pig lead,
Firewood, ironware, and cheap tin trays.[21]

Thus on the sea, as elsewhere, appearances count. The old freighter adapts itself best to a contemptible or even illicit cargo. In the latter case, social blame is added to aesthetic disapproval. This is the source of poetry in the "Ville de Frisco," which carries only forbidden freight, as depicted by Cendrars with a stark realism that approaches hallucination.

C'est une antique carcasse dévorée par la rouille.
Vingt fois réparée, la machine ne donne pas plus de
    sept à huit noeuds à l'heure.
Ce navire est exclusivement chargé de cercueils de
    Chinois décédés en Amérique et qui ont décidé de se
    faire enterrer dans la terre natale. . . .[22]

[It is an ancient carcass consumed by rust.
The engine, repaired twenty times, doesn't make
    more than seven or eight knots.
This ship is laden exclusively with coffins of Chinese
    deceased in America, who have decided to be buried
    in their native soil. . . .]

It would be hard to imagine anything more striking than this sordid community of living and dead on the remains of a ship engaged in crossing the vast Pacific. By a remarkable process of chameleon-like camouflage, the ship has taken on the character of its surroundings. The name of the freighter has been abbreviated, dropping the "San" ("Saint") which it must originally have had, and even the "Francisco" has been eroded to the point where it no longer has any human resemblance. Here we have mechanical civilization at its worst, and this should be enough to tempt Poseidon's

21. John Masefield, "Cargoes" in *Poems* (New York: The Macmillan Co., 1917).
22. *Kodak.*

brother, Hades, to snatch it from the kingdom of the Sea
into the kingdom of Death.   Moreover, this return to native
soil seems to draw with it a return to the sea-mother, and
this is a source of the poetic fatality of Cendrars' text.   In
dreams the sea is a living element, and whenever it is associated with death, the conjunction is a fruitful one.   Paul
Fort expresses excellently this twofold dialectic of the sea.
In "Fin marine" he wants to lose himself eternally in the
element, a favorite abode of death:

> là où le prime ne tremble jamais, où n'existent point
> nos amours de Mai, où, semée d'étoiles, ne brille la
> > vase
> que du phosphore épars des noyés en extase.[23]

[There where the prime never trembles, where our
loves of May have no existence, where the mud,
sown with stars, shines only with the scattered phos-
phorus of the ecstatic drowned.]

But on the contrary, in "Les grands courants des mers," he
sees the fruitful and maternal aspect of the sea.

> Je veux parler des grandes courbes de la Vie, de sa
> géometrie sur les Océans verts; de vagues déliées,
> volontaires, ravies, semant la Vie sur terre au vent
> de leurs grands gestes!

> Cette île a pris naissance en un lait ravissant, fait
> de flots veloutés, d'algues et d'éponges d'or, chaud au
> corail qui sourd et point dans l'air, vivant! et les
> palmiers ondoient sur les blancs madrépores.[24]

[I want to speak of the great curves of Life, of its
geometry on the green Oceans; unfettered, head-
strong, enraptured waves sowing Life over the earth
in the wind of their grand gestures.

23. *Ballades françaises* (Paris: Flammarion, 1925).
24. *Ibid.*, p. 111.

This island was born in a delicious milk made of velvety waves, algae and golden sponges, warm with coral which rises and sprouts in the air, alive! and the palm trees undulate over white madrepores.]

Given these two personalities, it is natural for the sea to appear a judge or arbiter par excellence. At Zeus' command, Poseidon unleashed the liquid element which soon covered all the earth except Parnassus, where Deucalion and Pyrrha were saved, and the archetype of the flood is an enduring one that we meet again, for example, in the story of Noah and the theme of Atlantis and the Breton village of Ys. Often the water is a mirror representing the border between the world of the living and the world beyond life, and from this arises its magic powers, of which there are many examples. We may cite the fountain of Truth in d'Urfé's *Astrée*, where faithful lovers find reflected the image of their beloved, while faithless lovers are devoured by the Lion and the Unicorn that guard it. Water, and especially the sea, is blended with the theme of death in a mystical, romantic, and retributive manner. This "Seascape" is built on such a mournful and grandiose variation.

> Over that morn hung heaviness, until,
> Near sunless noon, we heard the ship's bell beating
> A melancholy staccato on dead metal;
> Saw the bare-footed watch come running aft;
> Felt, far below, the sudden telegraph jangle
> Its harsh metallic challenge, thrice repeated:
> Standby. Half-speed ahead. Slow. Stop her!
>   They stopped.
> The plunging pistons sank like a stopt heart: . . .
> Burial at sea! . . .[25]

In the following scene, in which Louis MacNeice depicts the end of a freighter sent to the bottom by the enemy, we

25. Francis Brett Young, "Seascape" in *Second Selections from Modern Poets.*

meet again the rhythm of the same sinister progress toward
death, but accelerated as it approaches nothingness.

> Thus the wheel of the sea, of life, comes full circle,
>   the gun
> Swings in the swinging turret and finds her range
> To illuminate, to annihilate, in a flash
> Our timebound cargo and in a flash to change
> The morse of the mind to changelessness—dot and
>   dash
> Be ended and the circle and point be one.[26]

Beneath the surface of the sea, in fact, the dead belong
to another world. Even the imagination of Victor Hugo
seems to shy away from describing the sea's dead; he never
really answers the pathetic question he asks in "Oceano Nox."

> Où sont-ils, les marins sombrés dans les nuits noires?

> [Where are the sailors who went down in dark
> nights?]

It was not until the age of the submarine that man could
try to penetrate the mystery of the sea depths, which seemed
as forbidden as the depths of Hell from which so very few
had ever been able to return. From this strange world re-
vealed by the bathysphere and similar instruments, men
have come back with amazing visions, which poets like Supervielle have transcribed.

> Quand le groseillier qui pousse au fond des mers
> Loin de tous les yeux regarde mûrir ses groseilles. . .
> Quand l'eucalyptus des abîmes
> A cinq mille mètres liquides médite un parfum sans
>   espoir
> Des laboureurs phosphorescents glissent vers des
>   moissons aquatiques

26. "North Sea" in *Collected Poems: 1925-1948.*

Alors s'allument violemment les phares des pro-
    fondeurs
Qui sont violemment plus noirs que la noirceur
Et tournent—[27]

[When the currant bush growing at the bottom of
    the sea
Far from all eyes watches its currants ripen. . .
When the eucalyptus in the abyss
At five thousand liquid meters contemplates a per-
    fume without hope
Phosphorescent laborers glide toward aquatic harvests
Then the beacons of the depths, which are violently
    blacker than blackness,
Violently light up and turn. . . .]

There we have the phantasmagoric scenery of a dream, and
it is strange indeed to find another poet, an Englishman,
plunge into sleep as into the sea in a poem called "Bell, Pool
and Sleep."

The deep-sea bell of sleep
Under the pool of the mind
Flowers in concentric circles
Of annihilation till
Both sight and sound die out,
Both pool and bell are quelled.[28]

Thus the sea transcends the symbolic and becomes the
subconscious itself. The myth of the city under the sea is
parallel to the archetype of original sin, the source of guilt
feelings deep in our subconscious. The decisive moment in
the development of our profound personality was the period
when the realities of the phenomenal world were unable to

27. Jules Supervielle, "400 atmosphères" in *Gravitations* (Paris: Gallimard, 1932).
28. A. S. J. Tessimond, "Bell, Pool and Sleep" in *The Walls of Glass*
(London: Methuen, 1934).

weaken or deform the mysterious instinct, when the world was gentle and liquid, the period of life in the womb. Contemplation of the sea results, therefore, in a kind of splitting of the personality. Although all the anxiety of the human situation exists below the surface, there is joy in the movement of a modern ship which seems to fly over the waves. Guy Lavaud, a writer attracted to liquid imagery, shares with us all these emotions in a poem from a collection called *Sous le signe de l'eau:*

Sillage

Sur le monde si dur dorment les douces mers,
Comme sur les comptoirs les soies pâles et molles.
Parfois un grand steamer ainsi qu'un ciseau clair,
Rapide, coupe en deux la lueur de l'étoffe,
Et l'on voit s'évaser d'un bord à l'autre bord,
—L'une pour l'Amérique et l'autre pour l'Europe—
Deux lames bleues. . .[29]

[Over the rough world the gentle seas sleep,
Like pale, soft silks on a counter.
Sometimes a swift steamer, like a bright scissors,
Cuts the glimmering cloth in two,
And from one side to the other two blue waves
—One for America and the other for Europe—
Are seen to flare out. . . .]

The choice of feminine images gives this poem a gracefulness and airy harmony. Compared with the bottom of the sea, ships seem to fly in a triumph of unbroken movement. Verhaeren tells us that they skim over the surface of the water like thoughts over the surface of the subconscious.

De mer en mer, leurs vitesses entrecroisées,
Les navires s'en vont, pareils à des pensées.[30]

29. *Poétique du ciel* (Paris: Editions Emile-Paul Freres, 1930).
30. Emile Verhaeren, "La Conquête" in *Les Forces tumultueuses* (Paris: Mercure de France, 1915).

[From sea to sea, with intersecting speeds,
The ships fly on like thoughts.]

From a distance, all this is inspiring. The gigantic aesthetics
of the ship in its setting on the open sea, composed of fric-
tionless movement and horizontal grace, is a triumph of harmony which Luc Durtain expresses so well in "Norvège."

Le beau navire, blanc et bleu
Comme un nuage neuf, avance
    Aériennement;
L'embouchure de sa proue
Fait la rumeur d'un coquillage.[31]

[The beautiful ship, white and blue,
Like a new cloud, advances
    Aerially;
Her prow's mouth
Makes a sound like a sea shell.]

It is important to note, however, that all this joy proceeds
from the remote observation of the ship, from a post which
is probably not very different from that of the observer in
Valéry's "Le Cimetière marin."   When the poet is a pas-
senger on the ship, he cannot forget the mechanical heart-
beats of the engine. Sometimes he is content to model the
rhythm of his verse on the throbbing which ocean travelers
know so well.

L'*Armand-Behic* (des Messageries Maritimes)
File quatorze noeuds sur l'Océan Indien. . . .[32]

[The Armand-Behic (of the Maritime Shipping
    Lines)
Rides at fourteen knots on the Indian Ocean. . . .]

Often this measured movement forces the introduction of
rhythm, that is, time, with all it implies for the human
being.

31. *Kong Harald* (Paris: G. Crès, 1914).
32. H. J.-M. Levet, *Poèmes* (Paris: Gallimard, 1943).

But down the ladder in the engine-room
    (Doom, doom, doom, doom)
The great cranks rise and fall, repeat,
The great cranks plod with their Assyrian feet
To match the monotonous energy of the sea.[33]

Here we have the phenomenon of multiple incasements: the life of the machine within that of the hull within that of the sea. But the engine's life is personal, inscribed in time, and transmits itself to an immense mass which overlooks the modifications inflicted upon it. The beautiful wake of a ship is a perfect example of transience. Thus it seems that, since the disappearance of sails, the inspiration attached to ships encompasses both flight and the movement which, involving as it does fixed points of reference, is truly terrestial. Poets are excited by Neptunian dreams in which unhesitatingly they defy the taboo of the surface, or by the exaltation of a dream of flight, of skimming over the water. The former plunges us into the mysteries of the past, the latter into those of the future; the dialectic of the imagination in relation to the ship seeks its present between these two poles.

Les navires cherchent par tous les vents du monde,
Dans tous les ports et dans toutes les nuits,
Le soleil qui tombe des étoiles,
Le soleil qui monte des algues.[34]

[Ships seek, with every wind in the world,
In every harbor and in every night,
The sun that falls from the stars,
The sun that rises from the seaweed.]

This, in a striking abridgment, is the story of man's destiny, his search for a balance between the exterior future (*étoile*) and the stratification of the past within his consciousness

33. Louis MacNeice, "Passage Steamer" in *Poems, 1925-1940*.
34. G. Neveux, "Salut à l'escadre" in *La Beauté du Diable* (Paris: Gallimard, 1929).

(*algue*). Apollinaire was very conscious of this felicitous symbolism of the ship when he wrote:

> Mon beau navire ô ma mémoire
> Avons-nous assez navigué
> Dans une onde mauvaise à boire
> Avons-nous assez divagué
> De la belle aube au triste soir[35]

> [O memory, my beautiful ship,
> Have we sailed long enough
> In an ill-tasting wave
> Have we drifted long enough
> From fair dawn to sad evening?]

Havelock Ellis, in his chapter on "Aviation in Dreams," observes particularly that in dreams flying often takes the form of floating in air.[36] Air and water lend themselves to basically fluid reveries or daydreams, in contrast to the *monde dur* which Guy Lavaud mentions above.

Freud devotes many pages to dreams of flying, sketching for us what he considered the unacceptable theories of Stumpel (that dreaming of flight is an actualization of breathing) and of Federn (that dreaming of flight is dreaming of erection, to be compared with the winged phallus of the ancients). He thinks rather that the dream of flight is a bridge by means of which the dreamer identifies himself with a secret or shameful wish.[37] For these reasons the dream of flight is first of all that which enables one to do away with the necessary conditions of life, of which gravity is no doubt the most universal. Psychological experiments show that artificially induced sleep is often preceded by a dream of flight, especially in the case of anesthesia. It is interesting to see an English pilot reverse the process and pass from flight into a half-sleep.

35. "La Chanson du mal-aimé" in *Alcools*.
36. *The World of Dreams* (New York: Houghton & Mifflin, 1911).
37. Freud, *The Interpretation of Dreams*, pp. 364-71.

A sudden roar, a mighty rushing sound,
a jolt or two, a smoothly sliding rise,
a tumbled blur of disappearing sound,
and then all sense of motion slowly dies.
Quiet and calm, the earth slips past below,
as underneath a bridge still waters flow.

. . . .

And so I sit, half sleeping, half awake,
dreaming a happy dream of golden days. . . .[38]

The result is a total aerial pleasure and a return to the
dream of a Paradise Lost which we have always found in
moments of great exaltation.   These themes are present in
the poem Jean Cocteau devotes to his flights with the pioneer
of aviation, Rolland Garros, "Le Cap de Bonne-Espérance."

Péninsule
de hauteur

Prisonnier sur parole de la terre
à quatre mille de hauteur
à l'infini de profondeur

Un cerf-volant de ton enfance
soudain sans fil tu t'enracines
assis dessus[39]

[Peninsula of altitude

Prisoner of earth on parole
at a height of four thousand
at a depth of infinity

A paper kite of your childhood
suddenly without string you take root
seated on top]

38. Jeffery Day, "On the Wings of the Morning" in *Second Selections
from Modern Poets.*

39. Fraigneau, ed., *Cocteau pur lui-meme* (Paris: Editions du Seuil,
1957).

The dream is satisfying so long as it sustains itself, so long as the poet can forget his own body. This is the essential condition of the dream. The body is a bit of clay, a symbol of earth; let it reappear, and anxiety will seize the man in flight. It may not yet provoke a fall, but rather the terrible solitude of feeling cut off from everything, even from death. During the imaginary flight man can attain to the most nearly complete oblivion of self, especially if his machine is primitive enough not to seem like some sort of factory temporarily detached from the ground. Here is a vision of "Night Flying."

> [He] Sees in the misty deep a fainting light
> Of far-off cities cast in coal-dark bars
> Of shore and soundless sea; and he is lone,
> Snatched from the universe like one forbid,
> Or like a ghost caught from the clay and thrown
> Out on the void, nor God cared what he did.[40]

The sensation here is so acute that it becomes actually painful. The poet has not yet found the habitual security of flight.

With the depiction of the aerodrome, however, we attain plasticity. This is the triumph of the dream, of harmony, of untroubled calm; since the conquest is complete, peace returns. The aerodrome, in fact, lends itself to imagery which is much more aerial than that occasioned by flight itself. First, it offers a pole of comparison, a fixed point of reference, and then it is symbolic of successful flight. It shuts out the idea of that perpetual struggle against the air which Saint-Exupéry describes so well, for example, in *Night Flight*. Stephen Spender has written "The Landscape Near an Aerodrome"; man has not only conquered Aeolus, but has put him into service. There is no discord, only sweet and melodious sounds. The submissive earth awaits its con-

40. Frederick V. Branford, "Night Flying" in *Second Selections from Modern Poets*.

queror, the imaginary fall is regulated and becomes a controlled glide. It is the crowning accomplishment of the machine age, a victory as thoroughly acquired as that by which we breathe the vivifying air.

> More beautiful and soft than any moth
> With burring furred antennae feeling its huge path
> Through dusk, the airline with shut-off engines
> Glides over suburbs and the sleeves set trailing tall
> To point the wind. Gently, broadly, she falls,
> Scarcely disturbing charted currents of air.[41]

Now man can let himself go. In this twilight he can feel happy and at rest, because he has finished his work. He can feel victoriously aerial.

And now that flying has taken on a regular, human character, the individual can utilize it to his own ends, to celebrate love. Certainly this poem, "The Aeronaut to his Lady," is comical, but the surprise may reasonably provoke more serious emotions.

I

Through
Blue

Sky
Fly

To
You

Why?
Sweet

Love

Feet

Move

So
Slow.[42]

41. *Collected Poems: 1928-1953* (New York: Random House, 1955).
42. *More Verse by F.S.* (London: Sidgwick & Jackson, 1923).

It is also true that flying has another relation to humanity in general: aerial bombardment, a principal cause of the great fear of the twentieth century. Many poets have hesitated to take up a theme so common it has become trivial, and yet what forceful evocations it can produce.

> And over us a sound of humming,
> —Of hornets or bad bees a-bumming!
> A devilish, strident, hoarse, discordant
> Whirring of dark fliers mordant—
> My soul stands still and sweats with fear.[43]

The notion of retributive or poetic justice is here implied. By flying, man has violated the laws of destiny. He has deserted the legitimate place assigned him by nature, and he must pay for it. If we accept the doctrine of Freud, the dream of flight represents a desire inadmissable during our waking hours, and it is therefore also a manifestation of sin which must be punished. In another sense, flight is an open defiance of the gods, since man lays claim to a power which only they should have. We find this idea of poetic justice in Philippe Desportes' sonnet "Icare," written in the second half of the sixteenth century.

> Icare est cheut icy, le jeune audacieux,
> Qui pour voler au ciel eut assez de courage;
>
> .   .   .   .
>
> Il mourut poursuivant une haute aventure;
> Le ciel fut son désir, la mer sa sépulture:
> Est-il plus beau dessein ou plus riche tombeau?[44]

> [Icarus, audacious youth, who had enough courage
> To fly to the sky, fell here. . .
> He died in pursuit of a high adventure;
> Heaven was his desire, the sea his grave:
> Is there a more beautiful purpose or a richer tomb?]

43. Herbert Palmer, "Air Raid" in *Collected Poems* (London: Benn, 1933).
44. *Anthologie de la poésie française.*

Thanks to the machine, today flight does not ordinarily end in a fall, and a real psychological disequilibrium is the result. Here again man has advanced more rapidly on the scientific than on the moral level. The offense to heaven is as great, but man's technical ability permits him to avoid immediate punishment. Heaven's revenge takes the form of a spiritual disorder which Ivan Goll translates well in the following series of images:

> Sur les ailes d'un zéphir pneumatique
> Je plane poète plus lourd que l'air
> Vers un soleil nickelé qui bout à bain-marie
> Sur les brouillards. . . .[45]

> [On wings of a pneumatic zephyr
> I soar poet heavier than air
> Toward a nickle-plated sun boiling
> In the waterbath over the fogs. . . .]

And this disorder extends from the individual to society. Icarus was struck down for his daring, and the Tower of Babel, another attempt to conquer the sky, only brought about one more of the calamities which humanity suffered for being too bold. Today's equivalent of Babel's destruction is bombardment, which constitutes a perfect hell because the executioners suffer and die as well as their victims. A heart-breaking example is this piteous autobiography titled "The Death of the Ball Turret Gunner."

> From my mother's sleep I fell into the State,
> And I hunched in its belly till my wet fur froze.
> Six miles from earth, loosed from its dream of life,
> I woke to black flak and the nightmare fighters.
> When I died they washed me out of the turret with
> a hose.[46]

45. Ivan Goll, *op. cit.*
46. Randall Jarrell in *The Oxford Book of American Verse*.

Here we have the poignant beauty of ancient tragedy. The
State is a blind god who tears the infant from his mother and
sends him to a terrifying death. The last line especially is
charged with the heavy and sardonic fatality of idolatrous
sacrifice. This is realized by the three-fold transformation
of water: maternal water, which engenders ("my mother's
sleep"), water which kills ("wet fur froze"), and finally
the indifferent, antiseptic water which washes and removes.
How true it is that "water is the universal symbol of subconscious life."[47]   From the aesthetic point of view, this
represents the three stages of a descent into servility. The
innocent individual is seized unexpectedly—for how could
he suspect an element of life to change into a principle of
annihilation?—and this produces a lasting impression of
sadism and pity by making us respond to a beauty analogous
in its make-up to that of certain works of Villon—for example,
the ballad he wrote in jail when he expected to be hanged.

> Frères humains qui après nous vivez,
> N'ayez les cueurs contre nous endurcis. . .
>
> [Brother humans who live after us,
> Do not harden your hearts against us. . . .]

The fifteenth-century poet could hope for God's for-
giveness and eternal salvation, but the poets of our day see
only the death of the soul in store for the inhabitant of a
mechanical world. The hell of bombardment is only the
last step in the despiritualization of man evoked by Louis
MacNeice in the tragic poem called "Swing-Song" from
which these lines are taken.

> I'm only a wartime working girl,
> The machine shop makes me deaf,
> I have no prospects after the war
> And *my* young man is in the R.A.F.

47. C. Baudouin, *De l'instinct à l'esprit* (Bruges: Desclée de Brouwer,
1950), p. 197.

K for Kitty calling P for Prue. . .
Bomb Doors Open. . .
Over to You.[48]

Primitive man frankly distrusted these fluids which, if one was not careful, were likely to carry off the soul, when one left one's mouth open too long, for example.[49] Modern man tries to combat and dominate the fluid; he is skillful enough to succeed temporarily, but vengeance follows soon after. Victory is never fully assured; it must always be rewon, and at such a price that it may reasonably be questioned whether the victory is worthwhile.

48. *Collected Poems, 1925-1948.*
49. Frazer, *op. cit.*, p. 180.

6.

The Black Magic of the Modern World

Now THAT WE HAVE depicted the reactions of poets to the various conquests of the machine, reactions which are far from being uniformly favorable or admiring, we shall present their attitude to industrial progress. The advance of technical improvement is something like an army on the march; if it is interesting to see the countries through which it marches, to envisage the possible direction of new offensives and the destruction and glory they involve, it is no less useful to observe its operations, its morale, its organization, and its strategy.

In its spiritual make-up, the society witnessing the triumph of the machine is very different from the one which preceded the industrial revolution. We have a tendency to be crudely ultra-scientific. Our changing civilization finds its most adequate expression in that ephemeral literature constituted by newspapers and glossy magazines. Finally, it may be said that the major part of our most representative pleasures find their greatest development at popular levels. These modifications of the atmosphere in which we live are important. They lead us to inquire whether modern man is capable of adjusting to the new social context he has created without debasing himself, and we turn anxious eyes toward the future, that is, toward civilizations which seem to be ahead of us in Europe—in particular, to the United States.

Clearly, these matters will be the concern of our reflective poets, of our contemporary Vignys and the like. We may well mention Vigny, for the ivory tower—in the sense in which he understood it—is impossible today, since rejection or refusal in itself has become an eloquent position to adopt. Certainly all human societies have their faults, but those of our machine age threaten to change man to such an alarming degree that the poet often feels he has a stern obligation not to turn his back on what is happening to humanity.[1]

Since scientists have become the high priests of the modern world, the masses enjoy plunging into pseudo-science. Magazines which claim to reveal the secrets of mechanics, of physics, of chemistry, even of medicine—effortlessly, and to everyone—flourish in our society. When Romains shows us the success of a Dr. Knock, whose scientific knowledge is based on the assimilation of pharmaceutical prospectuses, he intends much more than an enormous joke; he is putting his finger on one of the sore spots of our society. The fault certainly goes far back, as far back as Eve who first tasted the fruit of the tree of knowledge. Molière ridiculed doctors and the *femmes savantes,* and the eighteenth century's rage for the *cabinet scientifique* is well known. Doubtless the number of imaginary invalids increases in proportion to the number of illnesses, and perhaps even in proportion to the number of medicines, whose growth is even more rapid. If the theories of Pasteur have effected many cures in the hands of true scientists, they have given rise among the masses to a phantasmagoria of evil and impure powers. An ethical treatise could be written on the subject of prophylaxis; the more people insist on pasteurization, on disinfection, on aseptic packaging and the like, the less confidence they have in their fellow men, and the more they tend toward primitive man's world of fear. Therefore it is good to see a joyous spirit, who was also a delightful poet, Raoul Ponchon, try

1. This idea is developed in Stephen Spender's article, "Poetry and Politics," in *Penguin Progress, No 13.*

to dissipate these fears imposed by a too exact and too much respected art of medicine on the crowd of potential invalids.

La Salade

Echinocoque, trichocéphale-dispar,
Anguillule, amoeba coli, lombricoïde
Ascarides, ankylostome nicobar,
Oxyure vermiculaire, balantide. . .
J'en passe et des meilleurs. Tels sont, mes chers en-
        fants,
Entre mille autres, qui vivent à nos depens,
Les vers intestinaux, les monstrueux reptiles,
Sans compter les crochus et virguleux bacilles,
Qui rongent, sapent, scient, sucent nos intestins,
Quand nous faisons intervenir, dans nos festins,
Ce que vous appelez, moi de même, salade. . . .[2]

[Echinococcus, trichocephalus-dispar
Anguillulus, amoeba coli, lombricoid,
Ascaridae, ankylostome nicobar,
Oxyuris vermiculaire, balantide. . .
And I skip over the best. Such my dear children,
Among a thousand others living at our expense,
Are the intestinal worms, monstrous reptiles,
Not to mention the hooked and comma bacilli,
Which gnaw, sap, saw, and suck our intestines,
Whenever we introduce into our feasts
That which you call, as I do, a salad. . . .]

This witty indictment, inspired by newspaper articles attacking the innocent salad, has an English counterpart in a poem titled "Britannica Salt," from which the following lines are taken:

Life's little worries and business stress
Result, as we know, in biliousness;

2. *La Muse au cabaret* (Paris: Fasquelle, 1926).

Society now corrects this fault
With a couple of glasses of water-salt;
They substitute for wicked wine
Two tumblers full of innocent brine,
Or into H_2O they pour
An ounce and a half of sodium chlor.[3]

Not even sleep is exempt from this pseudo-scientific intrusion, and we owe to Tristan Tzara this strange description of a subconscious mind as light as it is inflammable:

Au lac d'hydrogène ramassé au sexe du sommeil
les cigarettes crient de petits oiseaux courent après
le rythme des moteurs c'est-à-dire ondulation dei
sospiri.[4]

[At the hydrogenous lake gathered at the sex of sleep
cigarettes cry little birds run after the rhythm of
motors that is to say undulation of sighs]

Whether on the surrealist plane or the more intelligible logical one, the protest is the same. It always assumes, and rightly so, that the evil has been done. Even more sober minds are subject to the contagion of "science-fiction," which has overrun the atomic age and literally soars in the air with visions that make those of Jules Verne and H. G. Wells seem like child's play. Certainly there have been thoughtful writers to cry danger and give solemn warnings, especially on the scientific and social levels, e.g., Aldous Huxley in *Brave New World*, and George Orwell in *Animal Farm* and *1984*. It is worth noticing that "science" of this highly colored, comic-strip variety does not seem to attract poets. It demands, to be sure, a fictional continuity like that of a detective story, a condition which would repel the most solid inspiration. In our day few poets anticipate; on the contrary,

3. *More Verse by F.S.*
4. "Atrocités d'Arthur Trompette et scaphandrier" from *L'Antitête* in *Poètes d'aujourd'hui*, Vol. 32.

they let themselves be pushed by scientific events and are content to react from time to time by evoking the behavior of their fellow men. At the half-way point of our century, the future no longer inspires poets because it is fundamentally dehumanized. By this we refer to the process already begun by means of which minds lose their individuality. Standardization destroys the love which used to be directed toward objects (what truly modern mind could understand Diderot's feelings for his old dressing gown?). A little more than a century after Lamartine's evocation of Milly, his native village,

> Objets inanimés, avez-vous donc une âme
> Qui s'attache à notre âme et la force d'aimer?

> [Inanimate objects, have you then a soul
> Which clings to our soul and forces it to love?]

we can observe that inanimate objects have lost their souls, and the process now extends to human beings. It is no accident that C. G. Jung has written a book called *Modern Man In Search of a Soul*. There are many reasons for this evolution, but first and foremost is the influence of mechanized means of propaganda. In the first rank of these is that huge corruption of the printed word, the newspaper.

Certainly there still exist daily and weekly newspapers which offer thoughtful material, but they are slowly retreating before the irresistible tide of the popular press which never makes any demand on the intelligence and which assures its readers the comfort of predictable reactions, in no way different from the conditioned reflexes which Pavlov inculcated in his animals. Siegfried Sassoon, anticipating the years to come, writes a scathingly ironic poem attacking the great press of the future, "Lines Written in Anticipation of a London Paper Attaining a Guaranteed Circulation of Ten Million Daily":

Primeval days were dull. Events existed
As unexploited masses of material.
Wars, plagues, and famines functioned unassisted,
And there was no synopsis to the serial.[5]

The characteristic of a great newspaper is, in fact, the technical exploitation of an event which proceeds to transform it into something that immediately captures the attention and then is easily digested. This procedure explains the growing importance of headlines in comparison to the stories they introduce. However, facts sifted through the popular press tend to become standardized.

The explosion of a bomb
The submarine—a burst bubble filled with water—

.   .   .   .

We know things from rotating machines
from flanges stamping, cutting, unrolling sheets from
   rolls. . . .[6]

Here we meet again the same infernal cycle which the machine seems to impose on man. The standardization of news results in boredom; therefore, the sensational must be found, and this, when it becomes dull in its turn, provokes a demand for the still more sensational, and so it goes. The result is an unhealthy probing, not for truth, but for imaginative movement from the possible to the impossible. And when this is brought about, the imagination is driven to still greater efforts of inventiveness, and these efforts are too often their own excuse for being. In industry, the design of automobiles is a good example of this movement. Their standardization resulted in concentration on superficial detail, useless in terms of performance, such as fins, grillwork, and the like. As these too are generally accepted throughout the industry, more imagination must be exercised, and func-

5. *Collected Poems* (London: Faber & Faber, 1947).
6. Stephen Spender, "Perhaps" in *Collected Poems*.

tional necessity is even further ignored. Too often in the
industrial effort, probability and potentiality—two very elastic
ideas—are substituted for facts. T. S. Eliot stigmatizes these
tendencies in Part V of his poem "The Dry Salvages," which
begins thus:

> To communicate with Mars, converse with spirits,
> To report the behavior of the sea monster,
> Describe the horoscope, haruspicate or scry,
> Observe disease in signatures, evoke
> Biography from the wrinkles of the palm
> And tragedy from fingers; release omens
> By sortilege, or tea leaves, riddle the inevitable
> With playing cards, fiddle with pentagrams
> Or barbituric acids, or dissect
> The recurrent image into pre-conscious terrors—
> To explore the womb, or tomb, or dreams; all these
>   are usual
> Pastimes and drugs, and features of the press. . . .[7]

In this way the worst kind of mythology is created, one
which is not justified by any faith whatever. Let us take
a general example. In almost all religions there is a principle of Good and a principle of Evil, e.g., Ormazd and Ahri-
man in ancient Persian Zoroastrianism. This dichotomy
reflects a constant tendency of the human spirit and offers a
simple solution to the most complicated problems. This
mental habit, grounded in faith, led man in principle to draw
near to the angels by fleeing the devil. Naturally there were
still wicked and criminal men, but nonetheless this simplifica-
tion contained an *a posteriori* justification which gave it value.

The modern press has seized on this distinction which now
corresponds to faithful readers (good) and non-readers
(bad). For a modest sum, anyone may purchase the drug by
which he is counted among the just. The element that fixed
true value has disappeared, for the goal is dishonestly at-

7. *Four Quartets.*

tained without effort. And finally the great modern newspaper is a mechanized enterprise of spiritual desecration. There is in all of us an Asmodeus complex; we all have a desire to act like the character in Le Sage's *Diable boîteux*, to take the roofs off houses, to discover their most intimate secrets. This is anti-social. The English law called "Peeping Tom" is still in force after nine centuries, and it punishes at the individual level what the newspapers are licensed to do on a grand scale. If a modern Lady Godiva were to ride through Coventry dressed only in her flowing hair, reporters from all the great newspapers would be assigned to photograph her. To see without being seen is in the dream world a manifestation of superiority; the "voyeur" vicariously experiences what the person observed has the weakness to do physically. This feeling of superiority explains the popularity in science-fiction of the theme of the invisible man and his power, which was always an attribute of the gods. The reader, penetrating into the intimacy of real heroes, lives by proxy, in a waking dream made by others. The most marked result of this is a pyramiding passivity, and it is doubtless for this reason that André Breton remarks, in his poem on the birth of poetry called "Sur la route de San Romano," that

> L'acte d'amour et l'acte de poésie
> Sont incompatibles
> Avec la lecture du journal à haute voix[8]

> [The act of love and the act of poetry
> Are incompatible
> With reading a newspaper aloud.]

Finally photography comes to crown the cult of nonthinking. Here again there is a perversion, a means of letting us see without using words, which allows the return to the primitive ideogram represented by the illustrated papers.

8. *Poètes d'aujourd'hui*, Vol. 18.

Photography becomes a means of filling printed space while reducing the text which is tiring to read. It is easy to understand the surprise of Jean-Richard Bloch, who finds a pearl in all this slime, his "Idée d'un nageur."

> Je t'ai trouvé dans un journal de sport,
> Un vulgaire journal de salon de dentiste,
> Parmi cent photos bêtes
> De cyclistes au thorax concave,
> De boxeurs naïvement soufflés,
> De managers à mâchoire de grenouille,
> D'escrimeurs cérémonieux et gantés.
>
> La page tournée, ton image est apparue en riant
> Dans la pose éternelle que tu avais su prendre
> Et qui te permettait d'attendre
> Pendant l'éternité, s'il l'avait fallu,
> Que j'aie tourné cette page et t'aie reñcontré,
> Jeune nageur américain, dans ce magazine français.[9]
>
> [I found you in a sports' magazine
> A popular magazine for a dentist's waiting room,
> Among a hundred stupid pictures
> Of cyclists with concave chests,
> Of boxers childishly panting,
> Of managers with frog-like jaws,
> Of ceremonious, gloved fencers.
>
> Turning the page, I saw your smiling picture
> In the eternal pose which you knew to take
> And which would allow you to wait
> Through eternity, if necessary,
> Until I had turned the page and found you,
> Young American swimmer in that French magazine.]

Our press faithfully reflects the fact that public sports are today financial enterprises—a far cry from their most beauti-

9. *Anthologie des poètes de la N.R.F.*

ful expression in the Olympic Games and their celebration of the human body dedicated to Zeus. In England J. C. Squire describes the crowd attending "The Rugger Match" between Oxford and Cambridge:

> The walls make a funnel, packed full; the distant gate
> Bars us from inaccessible light and peace.
> Far over necks and ears and hats, I see
> Policemen's helmets and cards hung on the ironwork:
> "One shilling," "No change given," "Ticket holders
>   only."[10]

And this is one of the characteristic episodes of Montherlant's "Critérium des novices amateurs."

> *Time*
> Douce est l'eau sur son corps qui brûle et sa vie
>   partout appuyée.
> Les trois cordes posent leurs trois ombres sur les
>   vertèbres de l'échine mouillée,
> blanche, imberbe, et reflétante comme le pur ivoire
>   césarien.
> Tout autour que devient la France? Mais ici vraiment
>   on est très bien.
> Ce quelque chose de déboutonné, sans une pensée, que
>   reposant!
> Et pas de pli au pantanlon et le col mou et pas de
>   gants.
> J'ai laissé l'*Action Française* à ma place et mon voisin
>   lit le *Populaire*.
> Ça ne fait rien, on est copains tout de même, il s'en
>   fait pas pour ça, le frère.
> Que de plaisir![11]

10. *Poems in One Volume* (London: William Heinemann Ltd., 1926).
11. *Les Onze devant la porte dorée: Deuxième Olympique* (Paris: Grasset, 1924). (*L'Action française:* extreme right-wing newspaper between the wars; *Le Populaire:* a socialist newspaper.)

[*Time*

Sweet is the water on his burning body and his life
    leaning everywhere.

The three ropes cast three shadows on the vertebrae
    of his damp spine,

White, hairless, reflecting like pure Caesarian ivory.

All around, what is happening to France? But here
    really, everything is swell.

This unbuttoned comfort, without a thought—how
    restful!

No crease in the trousers, a soft collar, and no gloves.

I left the *Action Francaise* on my seat and my neigh-
    bor reads the *Populaire*.

It doesn't matter, we're still pals, he isn't going to
    get upset about that, my brother.

What pleasure!]

These two texts complement one another admirably. The first indicates the existence of a crowd in the "unanimiste" sense, and the second shows how this crowd, identifying itself with the artificial event, succeeds in forgetting itself in collective esctasy. We have seen the manner in which modern man seeks to avoid spiritual contact with himself; through commercial sports he avoids at the same time bodily contact with others. He conquers or yields through the intermediary of another, whom he pays to play in his stead. He derives a feeling of pleasure or pride with no effort to himself. The action he enjoys is his by proxy only. Today's sports symbolize very well the infection which the machine age slowly insinuates into the arteries of mankind. And its influence is multiplied by the motion pictures. For technical reasons, it is easy to film a planned sporting event, and in addition to this there is the certainty that such films will be commercially successful because the crowd in a movie house quickly identifies itself with the one in a stadium through a common process of mental imitation.

If we are spared the trouble of exercising our muscles thanks to the business of sports, thanks to motion pictures we are spared the trouble of dreaming. The screen dreams for us. This is the theme of C. Day Lewis' long poem titled "Newsreel."

> Enter the dream-house, brothers and sisters, leaving
> Your debts asleep, your history at the door:
> This is the home for heroes, and this loving
> Darkness a fur you can afford.
>
> Fishes in their tank electrically heated
> Nose without envy the glass wall: for them
> Clerk, spy, nurse, killer, prince, the great and the
>   defeated
> Move in a mute day-dream.[12]

We find here the same danger we discovered before. The cinema, with its colors and animated cartoons, becomes for our society in some ways what stained-glass windows were for the people who built cathedrals. The principles are the same, our technique is superior, but faith is lacking. If, to employ the famous dictum, religion is the opiate of the people, we have no choice but to recognize that today when religion has disappeared as the overwhelming influence on social life, the opiate is left. The cinema is no doubt as frequented today as churches were in the ages of intense faith. When the service was ended, the flock were left with a soul-filling light; when the film is over, modern man falls back into his dreary oblivion. Since the poet is essentially a dreamer who invents images, he naturally feels no enthusiasm for this imagination by proxy. It is worth noticing how an English poet discreetly avoids the issue by praising the magic of the light (and not of the film).

12. *Collected Poems* (London: Jonathan Cape & The Hogarth Press, 1954).

Cinema Screen

Light's patterns freeze:
Frost on our faces.
Light's pollen sifts
Through the lids of our eyes. . . .[13]

And Pierre Albert-Birot tries to do the same thing by means
of unexpected verbal pirouettes.

Il y a des gens qui passent dans la projection
Et qui ne sont pas éclairés cor cor encore accord
Sous les sous les sons sont saoûls suçons
Personne n'a jamais vu le moteur qui produit la
    lumière
Ils sont bien obligés quelque fois de devenir humains
Le petit oiseau mangera le serpent
Noir et blanc le projecteur est sur l'autre trottoir. . . .[14]

[There are people who walk into the beam of light
And who are still not lighted. . .
No one has ever seen the motor which produces light
Sometimes they are obliged to become human
The little bird will eat the snake
Black and white the projector is on the other side-
    walk. . . .]

It may be thought that such a disconcerting form is inappro-
priate to the seriousness of the theme. Max Jacob especially
feels the danger so acutely that he renounces his usual fan-
tastic expression to give us a nearly regular text in "Printemps
et Cinématographie mêlés."

Ce soir, je vais au Cinéma. . .
Au son d'une musique absurde,
Nous verrons défiler des Kurdes, . . .[15]

13. A. S. J. Tessimond, "Cinema Screen" in *The Walls of Glass.*
14. "Cinéma" in *La Joie des sept couleurs* (Paris: Editions Sic, 1919).
15. *Anthologie de la poésie française.*

[This evening I'm going to the movies. . .
To the sound of absurd music
We'll see the Kurds march by]

And Robert Desnos, in a scathing parody of a certain species of film, destroys a celebrated hero of the screen with ridicule in "Complainte de Fantômas."

Ecoutez . . . faites silence
La triste énumération
De tous les forfaits sans nom,
Des tortures, des violences
Toujours impunis, hélas!
Du criminel Fantômas.[16]

[Listen . . . quiet please
For the sad enumeration
Of all the nameless crimes
Of torture, of violence,
Always unpunished, alas!
Of the criminal Fantomas.]

We must note, however, that these protestations are becoming rarer and rarer. At the extreme opposite, Karl Shapiro does not hesitate to sing the glories of "Hollywood" in an apology which ends thus:

What is more nearly ours? If soul can mean
    The civilization of the brain,
This is a soul, a possibly proud Florence.[17]

But unhappily the poet himself seems to be intoxicated, since he has apparently forgotten that ten lines earlier in the poem he expressed forcibly the dangers of this "civilization."

Here all superlatives come true
And beauty is marketed like a basic food.

16. *Poètes d'aujourd'hui*, Vol. 16.
17. *The Oxford Book of American Verse.*

No doubt it is to this world engendered by the films that Wallace Stevens alludes when he remarks bitterly in the refrain of one of his poems:

The only emperor is the emperor of ice-cream.[18]

Another child of progress, the radio, seems on the contrary to benefit from the prestige conferred by the conquest of space. The invention is so exciting that poets seem to concentrate on the victory it represents. Naturally Verhaeren finds a warm, engaging, lyrical expression.

Un fil d'airain chargé de sonores paroles
Vibre dans l'étendue—et les pensers s'envole
De l'un à l'autre bout de l'univers dompté. . . .[19]

[A brass wire charged with sonorous words
Vibrates in space—and thoughts fly
From one end of the tamed world to the other. . . .]

Drieu la Rochelle gives us in "T.S.F." a poem based on the music of the call for help and on the philosophical grandeur of this instantaneous communication.

—Vous, vous, vous,
D'autres hommes
Quelqu'un sur la terre
Nos paroles se dissolvent dans le silence du ciel.[20]

[—You, you, you,
Other men
Someone on earth
Our words melt away into the silent sky.]

However, with the passing of time, wonder and amazement diminish. There is already something disturbing in these lines by Pierre MacOrlan.

18. "The Emperor of Ice Cream" in *ibid.*
19. "La Conquête" in *Les Forces tumultueuses.*
20. *Fond de cantine* (Paris: Gallimard, 1920).

Tel était Paris avec sa grande tour où, chaque nuit,
    crépite la chevelure bleue de la T.S.F.
et ses étincelles qui laissent sur le mur de la nuit
des traces d'allumettes chimiques. . .[21]

[Such was Paris with its great tower where, every
    night, the blue tresses of radio sputter
and its sparks which leave traces like chemical matches
on the wall of night. . . .]

And we begin to have serious doubts in reading "T.S.F." by
Emmanuel Aergeter.

Un prêtre a rapproché Daventry dans ses brumes;
Illuminant le pur Zodiaque des voix,
    Les lampes s'allument:
    Le globe est à moi. . .

J'entends Java brûlante au disque qu'elle emprunte,
Un menuet de Grieg qui chante sous la neige. . .
    Mais la voix défunte,
    Un soir l'entendrai-je?[22]

[A priest has brought Daventry closer in its fog;
Illuminating the pure zodiac of voices,
    Lamps light up:
    The globe is mine. . . .

I hear sun-baked Java on a borrowed record,
A minuet by Grieg singing under the snow. . .
    But that dead voice,
    Shall I hear it one evening?]

The conquest of the ether is not accompanied by a victory
over the other world which still eludes us. Radio pours over
the entire planet the bad taste which reigns in many pro-
grams; it causes such a consumption of ideas and themes

21. "Inflation sentimentale" in *Poésies documentaires complètes* (Paris:
Gallimard, 1954).
22. *Le Voilier aux diamants* (Paris: Houala, 1935).

that the supply cannot be sufficient; and every day it is
tempted more and more to surrender itself to vulgarity.
Like all habits, it has finally become second nature.   This
accounts for the sale of portable radios which enable those
who cannot break the habit to abandon themselves to it wherever they are.   Has this increased human happiness?   Is
there any compensation for the burden of this added subjec-
tion?   This "Escalade" spoken by a government employee
encourages our doubts.

> . . . les machines à écrire bégayent
> et le téléphone insiste
> Est-ce que je vais savoir encore courir
> la gare n'est pas loin
> un tramway rampe jusqu'à Versailles
> On m'avait dit qu'il y avait un accident tout près d'ici
> je ne pourrai donc pas entendre le hennissement des
>   nuages
> La Tour Eiffel lance ses rayons aux Iles Sandwich
>
> Gutenberg 24-19[23]
>
> [. . . typewriters stutter and the telephone insists
> Shall I still know how to run?
> The station isn't far away;
> A streetcar runs to Versailles.
> They told me there was an accident right near here
> So I shan't be able to hear the clouds whinnying.
> The Eiffel Tower shoots its beams to the Sandwich
>   Islands.
>
> Gutenberg 24-19.]

As for the telephone, it is considered a burden which
foists itself upon us when it is not wanted, and Tristan Tzara
discovers this disturbing metaphor for it: "The telephone
remains faithful to us like a nickel dog.[24]

23. Philippe Soupault, "Escalade" in *Rose des vents* (Paris: Au Sans
Pareil, 1920).
24. "Escalade" in *Poètes d'aujourd'hui*, Vol. 32.

Certainly a counterpart of this progress has been the facility with which mechanical sound can be reproduced ad nauseum, always to the same end of preventing men from thinking. In a poem titled by a fateful date, "September 1, 1939"—a day when the American man in the street ought to have tried to make some mental effort—Auden shows us how modern man is brutalized by noise—for what else can we call that mechanical music which, whether we like it or not, assails our ears?

> Faces along the bar
> Cling to their average day:
> The lights must never go out,
> The music must always play. . . .[25]

Whether we accept or indignantly reject it, the result is the same. The mechanical process imposes itself. We say mechanical process because the human voice recorded and then reinterpreted by the listener is only a system of acoustical writing. This applies to music as well, although in a less obvious manner, and it explains why the true lover of music always prefers to attend a concert rather than listen to one broadcast by radio, no matter how perfect the transmission may be. To the sensitive soul there is something in this deformation more tragic than silence itself.

> The megaphone-microphone-magnified voice of the
>   King
> Spoke hollow and careful from vacant remoteness
>   of air.[26]

The machine first uproots us, then overpowers us with an ersatz pleasure. The leisure it offers is based on disorder, on a state of trance when we are not our ordinary selves, produced by the extension of the effort of modern work into

25. W. H. Auden, *op. cit.*
26. Siegfried Sassoon, "Afterthoughts on the Opening of the British Empire Exhibition" in *Collected Poems*.

the void.   The radio and mechanical music do nothing but
satisfy a need for noise which the factory and the street have
created in the average man.   Still better adapted to the
satisfaction of this need are the amusement parks and dance
halls which continue the frenzied work-rhythm after work
is through.   It is remarkable to notice how dancing follows
the acceleration of production; there is as great a difference
between the minuet and rock-and-roll as between older
methods of manufacturing and today's assembly line.   There
is no place left for rest; when the body stops from exhaustion,
the mind continues its mad career.   This accounts for the
enormous consumption of aspirin and sleeping pills in "advanced" civilizations.   Machine-age man is a potential
schizophrenic.   That is why it would be a mistake to dis-
miss the wise nonsense of Max Jacob.

> Les manèges déménagent.
> Ménager manager
> De l'Avenue du Maine
> Qui ton manège mène
> Pour mener ton ménage! . . .[27]

> [The merry-go-rounds are moving out.
> Thrifty manager
> Of the Avenue de Maine
> You make your merry-go-round go 'round
> In order to feed your household.]

This idiotic mechanization of rhythm corresponds exactly
to reality.   Man is stultified, stupified, mechanized; industrial civilization triumphs over its creator.   An amusement park is no longer an "artificial paradise" like those
glorified by De Quincey and Baudelaire that could elicit a
fugitive but poetic ecstasy.   It has become an institution of
vain disorder:

27. *Poètes d'aujourd'hui*, Vol. 3.

Et depuis, du fougueux vainqueur,
  C'est, la course incongrue,
Un Scenic-railway qui se rue
  Aux tournants de mon coeur![28]

[And ever since, there's the strange race
  Of the fiery conquerer,
A scenic railway rushing
  In the turnings of my heart.]

And especially of that evil which cannot be described or complained of because its causes are too numerous to be analyzed exactly and because it strikes too many people for the poet to be able to incite pity in others. Pierre Morhange makes this diagnosis:

Encore mal dormi cette nuit
A cause du bal d'en face
Et à cause de ma vie.[29]

[Slept badly again last night
Because of the dance hall across the street
And because of my life.]

In all these descriptions of the amusement park there is no longer even a semblance of joy, nothing but the mournful routine of a feverish mechanism. The only ones who seem to have a good time are the friends of "Simone de Montmartre," who escape from factory life by selling themselves; thus for them mechanical pleasure is a change in the monotony of their lives.

Place Pigalle, jardin des lumières apprivoisées,
les femmes aux yeux brillants de publicité
courent sur les manèges comme les souris de la ruine.
Une merveilleuse escadre appareille
à travers les armatures de fer galvanisé.

---

28. Jean Pellerin, "Dédicaces" in *Le Bouquet inutile.*
29. "Epigramme" in *Anthologie des poètes de la N.R.F.*

.   .   .   .

Simone a payé sa place.
Elle grimpe sur le manège cabré comme un léopard.[30]

[Place Pigalle, garden of tame lights,
Women with eyes bright with advertising
Jump on the merry-go-rounds like mice of doom.
A marvelous squadron sets sail
Through the framework of galvanized iron. . . .
Simone has paid for her seat.
She climbs onto the merry-go-round which rears like
    a leopard.]

It is not surprising that poets turn to the gloomiest kind of humor to evoke the "Fête foraine."   Prévert's poem with this title ends:

Heureux le vieil idiot
Qui fracasse la vaisselle
Heureux dans son carrosse
Un tout petit enfant
Malheureux les conscrits
Devant le stand de tir
Visant le coeur du monde
Visant leur propre coeur
Visant le coeur du monde
En éclatant de rire. . . .[31]

[Happy the old idiot
Who shatters dishes
Happy the little baby
In its carriage
Unhappy the greenhorns
In front of the shooting gallery
Aiming at the world's heart

---

30. Pierre MacOrlan, "Simone de Montmartre" in *Poésies documentaires complètes.*
31. *Paroles.*

Aiming at their own heart
Aiming at the world's heart
And bursting into laughter. . . .]

But it is Montesquiou-Fezensac who has the final word with this appalling line which closes one of the quatrains of "Baraques":

La foule affreusement grouille.[32]

[The crowd swarms hideously.]

Where does this horror come from? To begin with, from the fact which we have already noted that the crowd is feminine. Jules Romains, in one of his early poems, cried:

Ne te défends pas, foule femelle,
C'est moi qui te veux, moi qui t'aurai![33]

[Don't draw away, female crowd,
It is I who want you, I who will have you!]

and there is a permanent and specacular transgression in the machinery of the carnival. Again we come across the complex which we have already studied in the city, but worse than it was before. The carnival is a machine which runs to no purpose, a factory with many people that produces nothing at all. Here we have the reductio ad absurdum of our problem; in every other instance the philosophy of the machine was a pragmatic one, and acquired utility was always invoked to justify every kind of disadvantage. In this particular case all real pragmatism has ceased to apply. We have the machine alone foisting itself on us to satisfy a need for rhythm and frenzied escape in the crowd of industry's servants. In the collectivized rhythm, the masses discover their "Mana" or artificial stimulus, whose difference from the "mana" of primitive tribes in their celebrations would

32. *Les Hortensias bleus* (Paris: Charpentier, 1896).
33. "Ode à la foule qui est ici" in *Odes et prières* (Paris: Gallimard, 1923).

be insignificant, if the so-called "civilized" crowds were not under the constant control of their police. This is the sign of a regression the real extent of which is difficult to measure, but which Pierre Reverdy evokes with consummate skill in his "Fête foraine."

> Le point de l'appareil montre le regard fixe
> Le regard
> Le hasard des mots
> venant du bout des doigts du monstre
> Le retard du lever de la toile
> Sous les lampes vides et presque mortes
> Dans le vent plein d'eau et de secrets.[34]

> [The point of the instrument shows the fixed look
> The look
> The accident of words
> Coming from the monster's finger-tips
> The delay in raising the curtain
> Under the empty and nearly dead lamps
> In the wind full of water and secrets.]

This possessive power exerted by a force of evil is staggering. To be sure, there are moments when real life thrusts itself forward, and the carnival is interrupted. Then the crowd regains some fragments of its soul—first of all its utility, and then its role in the universe.

The poet always takes pleasure in evoking the grandeur of the human race, since he thus indirectly celebrates his own. It is worth noticing that this crowd, which is the theme of the following poem by Carl Sandburg, lives within the imagination of the author. This permits a far greater liberty and enthusiasm than can be provided by direct contact, in which limitations always tend to crop up.

34. *Coeur de chêne* (Paris: Galerie Simon, 1921).

I am the people—the mob—the crowd—the mass.
Do you know that all the great work of the world is
    done through me?
I am the workingman, the inventor, the maker of the
    world's food and clothes.
I am the audience that witnesses history. The Na-
    poleons come from me and the Lincolns.
    They die. And then I send forth more
    Napoleons and Lincolns. . . .[35]

This enthusiasm seems to be a delayed Americon expression of the kind found in France at the time of Zola,
when the religion of science was at its height. Now, however, many poets are disillusioned and tend to cry over the
indifference of the masses when confronted by great events
like the death of lyricism:

The petrol pumps are doing a roaring business,
Motors are tuning up for the Easter races,
Building companies are loaning to the newly married—
    Pindar is dead and that's no matter.[36]

Here the technique of reviewing the facts approaches
that of newspaper reporting. This genre depends upon
objective exposition, omitting all attempt at explanation.
Vachel Lindsay, utilizing the same method, describes the
house-symbol of our society, the factory. Following the
rules of the genre, he fastens upon the significant detail.

Factory windows are always broken.
Other windows are let alone.
No one throws through the chapel-window
The bitter, snarling, derisive stone.[37]

And this is the focal point of the tragic misunderstanding.
The factory merits such hatred only because it is misunder-

35. "I am the People, the Mob" in *op. cit.*
36. Louis MacNeice, "Pindar is Dead" in *Poems, 1925-1940.*
37. "Factory Windows Are Always Broken" in *Collected Poems.*

stood. Men have unjustifiably wanted to raise it to the level of a church, and now they reproach it for not being worthy of such a designation. This is the whole drama of irrational generalization imposed by the masses. Perhaps to find a truth again, one must seek it among those individuals whose dynamism makes them leaders of the crowd, directing it and making it truly productive.

L'entraîneur

—Qui es-tu, qui es-tu?
—L'homme fier, à qui demain ne fait pas peur.
Aujourd'hui je vis de salaires; demain de rentes. . . .[38]

["Who are you?   Who are you?"
"The proud man unafraid of tomorrow.
Today I live on a salary, tomorrow on dividends."]

and the businessman depicted by E. E. Cummings in a poem with the evocative title "buy me an ounce and i'll sell you a pound."[39]

No doubt the most evident materialization of this double state of mind, the ability to lead and a flair for business, is advertising, that distinctive product of the modern world. We shall return to its verbal signification; from the material point of view, it is characterized by that appeal of the factitious which Ben Maddow depicts in

The City

. . . this city honors most the false:
The lady behind glass, untouched by human hand,
With plaster pubis, thigh and docile belly
Lifting the admired fabric up for sale—
While the living long to wear her enameled eyes.[40]

38. A. Spire, "L'entraineur" in *Versets* (Paris: Mercure de France, 1908).
39. *The Oxford Book of American Verse.*
40. *A Little Treasury of Modern Poetry* (London: Routledge & Kegan Paul, 1947).

This is exactly the trouble. The machine has preverted our souls to such a degree that it has managed to reverse the archetype. Our modern Galateas who are really alive aspire to become statues. Of their own accord they long for the mythical punishment of petrifaction, the retribution which was visited on Sodom and Gomorrah and the legendary horsemen who persecuted the early Christians and were turned into the menhirs of Carnac. Through a spiritual masochism which is very characteristic of our age, Hell is within ourselves and in our crowds. Even the angels are lured into the trap.

> Prenant pour des éclairs de Dieu
> La fausse lumière des hommes,
> Comment pourrait se méfier,
> L'Ange de notre magnésium?
> Le voilà photographié.[41]

> [Taking the false light of men
> For God's lightning
> How should an Angel
> Be on guard against our magnesium?
> There he is—photographed.]

But angels, like gods and all other creatures, resent being deceived, especially since their affair with Lucifer. The hypocrisy which deceives the Angel is Sin, whose origins go back to that original sin which is always present, though it has taken on new forms.

> Au Bar du Paradis Perdu
> Adam et Eve boivent du
> Porto-flip avec des pailles—
> Adieu les célestes ripailles. . .[42]

41. Raymond Radiguet, "Fragment d'une élégie" in *Les Joues en feu* (Paris: Grasset, 1925).
42. Mathias Lubeck, "Petit Poème postparadisiaque" in *Anthologie de la nouvelle poésie*.

[At the Paradise Lost Bar
Adam and Eve drink
Port-wine flips through straws—
Farewell the celestial feasts. . . .]

These poets who evoke sacred religious themes illustrate
the law of social psychology which explains that there is a
tendency to talk especially about things that are lacking.
This constitutes an extremely fruitful exercise in catharsis
which has been subtly analyzed by P. M. Schuhl,[43] but is
there really any hope of replacing the entire edifice of supra-
human faith with mere words? As for the opposite attitude,
more frequently practiced, its dangers are obvious. Trying
to make the masses forget their spiritual poverty by means of
mechanical propaganda is putting a void in the place of the
soul, a deadly sin which humanity would find hard to expiate.

On both sides the evil seems irremediable, for there is
little to choose between nothingness and empty words. Many
of our writers find this disturbing. Many European novelists
have gone to the United States to sound out the future, and
many poets have given us pictures of the machine age on the
other side of the Atlantic which we have studied here as the
themes came up. This abundant literature has created a myth
of America and caused the greatest confusion in our minds.
It seems to us, however, that André Salmon synthesizes all
these attitudes in his burlesque poem beginning "Ovanuna
croyait. . . ." First, naïve faith in the myth:

Ovanuna croyait qu'en Amérique
Il ne volait oiseau que mécanique.

[Ovanuna believed that in America
The birds that fly are mechanical ones.]

Then, after several lines of transition questioning our own
European civilization and focusing the problem more sharply,

43. Chap. XII, *op. cit.*

we have a sort of tremendous cosmic hoax, whose symbolic value is unsettling.

> Je t'apprendrai grâce au calcul différentiel
> Qu'en vérité les gratte-ciel
> Grattent si bien et au si juste endroit
> Que le ciel éclatant de rire,
> Crevant de joie,
> Fait, tous les quarante ans,
> Trembler la terre en éclatant,
> —ainsi tomba Frisco. . . .[44]

> [Thanks to differential calculus, I'll show you
> That in truth skyscrapers
> Scrape so well, and in so precisely the right place,
> That the heavens, bursting with laughter,
> Splitting their sides with joy,
> Make the earth tremble every forty years
> —Thus fell Frisco. . . .]

To "scrape the sky" is clearly to defy the gods who had given a solemn warning at the time of the attempt at Babel. This challenge calls down a grotesque vengeance which is tragic and grandiose because it comes from heaven, yet comic and contemptible because it is directed against the pretentious creatures of our little world.

44. *Le Livre et la bouteille* (Paris: Camille Bloch, 1920).

7.

The Poetry of the Machine: Value, Meaning, and Influence

WE USUALLY THINK that the novel is the literary genre par excellence of our industrial era since it is the most popular. From the point of view of style the popular novel is relatively easy because, for the public at large, it is the story which counts more than anything else. The modern poem rarely contains a dramatic narrative. It is sustained only by a succession of notations which must interest the reader and reverberate within him. This psychology of notations is utilized by the obscure authors of what is, in fact, the most popular genre of all, the newspaper headline. The *Daily Express*, for example, one of the English dailies whose headlines are most carefully prepared, prints more than four million copies of every issue. What novelist can pretend to be read every day by ten million people? Yet everyone reads the headlines.

True, literary esthetes will object that this is mere commercialism, vulgarization, or the like; but it is nonetheless true that the problems of headlining constitute a real discipline[1] and that the psychological problems involved are not fundamentally different from those posed by a large part of the poetry of the machine age. In fact the solutions

[1]. Heinrich Straumann, *Newspaper Headlines: A Study in Linguistic Method* (London: G. Allen & Unwin, 1935). The author cites sixteen books on his subject, ten published between 1920 and 1934.

proposed by headlining seem to us applicable in some respects to poetry.

The first rule is the psychic shock. Modern man is so constituted that his capacity for interest has been blunted. In like manner, country people whose lives are less filled with surprises are more concerned with ordinary affairs than city people. As Mauriac says, citing a particular instance, "Passion loses all its character in Paris. Everyday Phaedra seduces Hippolytus there, and not even Theseus bothers about it."[2] No one will challenge the truth of this remark. Only a shock of some sort is capable of rousing the individual who lives in the midst of machines. The easiest way to produce one is by means of the extraordinary, and this explains why the popular press accords such a large space to the unexpected, and especially to crime. It would be naïve to imagine that poetry totally repudiates this procedure. It is curious to note that newspaper headlines and poetic expressions have become abbreviated in similar degrees, with their impact inversely proportional to the number of words used to express their meaning.

In 1857, the *Morning Post* headlined the news of the Indian Mutiny thus:

> Great Revolt of The Bengal Troops.
> Massacre of English at Delhi.
> Proclamation of a Mogul Prince.[3]

In 1918, the news of the German armistice request was headlined in the *Daily Mirror*:

> Huns Ask Armistice.

Now, separated by an interval which is approximately the same, we have these two descriptions of twilight. Baudelaire, in "Harmonie du soir," tells us:

2. Cited by André Maurois, "François Mauriac," in *Etudes littéraires*, II (New York: Editions de la Maison Française, 1944), p. 13.

3. Straumann, *op. cit.*

Le soleil s'est noyé dans son sang qui se fige.[4]

[The sun has drowned in its clotting blood.]

while Apollinaire writes in "Zone":

Soleil cou coupe[5]

[Sun throat cut]

In both instances there is a reduction of approximately two-thirds.

Like journalists, some poets take pleasure in evoking crimes which appeal to the taste for horror and a certain sadism latent in every society.

John MacDonald found a corpse, put it under the sofa,
Waited till it came to life and hit it with a poker,
Sold its eyes for souvenirs, sold its blood for whiskey. . . .[6]

This is perhaps only a somewhat ponderous and grotesque development of a sensation Apollinaire exploits in this meaningful line from "Il y a":

Il y a à minuit des soldats qui scient des planches pour des cercueils[7]

[At midnight there are soldiers sawing boards for coffins.]

But it is relatively too simple to play with ideas which everyone knows so well, such as death. The shock may simply derive from the ludicrous surprise of the subject. This may be of a gratuitous nature, as in the famous poem by Charles Cros, "Le Hareng saur," which describes in detail the simple act of a man's climbing a ladder to hang a kippered herring on a string, and ends:

4. *Les Fleurs du mal.*
5. *Alcools.*
6. Louis MacNeice, "Bagpipe Music" in *Poems, 1925-1940.*
7. *Alcools.*

J'ai composé cette histoire—simple, simple, simple,
Pour mettre en fureur les gens—graves, graves,
        graves,
Et amuser les enfants—petits, petits, petits.[8]

[I made up this story—simple, simple, simple,
To enrage people who are—serious, serious, serious,
And to amuse children—little, little, little.]

Or the shock of surprise may be full of profound meaning,
like the terrible gliding into the beyond that marks the
"Bascule" of Pierre Reverdy, ending:

Et moi je tombe
    Ma raison
        glisse
Entre les lames sous le pont
Je vois l'autre côté du monde[9]

[And I am falling
    My reason
        slides
Between the waves under the bridge
I see the other side of the world]

Finally, it may be like the contempt shown by W. B. Yeats
for his own lack of inspiration in his earlier works.

My circus animals were all on show. . . .[10]

Here the effect is obtained by the contrast between the subject and the unusual symbol employed.   Lyric poets rarely
utilize such metaphors to convey their themes—imagine
Lamartine comparing Elvire and Graziella to circus animals
for a fuller appreciation of the shock effect—yet Yeats continues a little further on with an equally contemptuous
metaphor:

8. *Le Coffret de santal* (Paris: Lemerre, 1873).
9. *Poètes d'aujourd'hui*, Vol. 25.
10. "The Circus Animals' Desertion" in *Last Poems* (New York:
Macmillan, 1940).

In the foul rag-and-bone shop of the heart.

We know how newspapers utilize similar procedures and exploit the sensational. There is, for example, the opposition between society and the individual with its effect of unbalance and strangeness. Max Jacob ends his poem "Années pourries" (the "rotten years," referring to the late 'twenties) with the mysterious words "L'Ennemi du Genre Humain" (an expression like "Public Enemy No. 1," well known from newspapers), utilizing the English procedure of headlining by capitalizing all the important words. We may even find the news item of sordid, commonplace crimes and swindles, as in this quatrain by William Plomer:

> Through the traffic, down the side-street
>> Where an unfrocked parson thrives
> ("Palmist and Psychologist")
>> Cutting short unwanted lives. . . .[11]

Still another kind of shock is that of conjuring up strange places. Translations owe part of their success to this procedure. Akin to it is the age-old use of exotic proper names, such as in Racine's "La fille de Minos et de Pasiphaé," and the love of romantic poets for local color. Today, of course, there is a tendency to strike out even farther, and André Salmon begins Part III of his poem "Prikraz" with these words:

> Ossip Ossipovitch Apraxin
> De la petite noblesse du Gouvernement de
>> Toula. . . .[12]

> [Ossip Ossipovitch Apraxin
> From the gentry of the Government of Toula. . . .]

while the English poet Kenneth Allott develops the method by choosing names which are also symbols of science:

11. "A Ticket for the Reading Room" in *The Dorking Thigh* (London: Jonathan Cape, 1945).
12. *Carreaux* (Paris: Gallimard, 1928).

Ballet of Fahrenheit and Réaumur
The swarm of bees round time's thermometer. . . .[13]

The most immediate consequence of such methods is naturally the passing of words from one language to another. Wyndham Lewis ends poem XXIV of the collection *One-Way Songs* with these words:

It is noblesse oblige[14]

while Cendrars, for example, adopts "factorie" as the French equivalent of the English "factory" which is quicker and less awkward than the older French word "factorerie."[15]   A further advance in this direction is the pure and simple neologism composed on analogies of meaning and phonetics as the case demands.   Henri Michaux accomplishes the feat of writing poems which turn on such creations, like "Le grand combat" with this representative line:

Il l'emparouille et l'endosque contre terre.[16]

"Emparouiller," with its evocative sound, is probably a composite of "s'emparer de" ("to seize upon") and "écrabouiller" ("to crush"), and "endosquer" is a mischievous variation of "adosser" ("to back against"). As Fantasio felt like shedding his skin, the modern poet feels like shedding his vocabulary and, in the present instance, seems to accomplish it perfectly. The reader is surprised; this unexpected decoding is a problem which attracts and amuses without discouraging him, because he arrives easily at the solution. Strangely enough it seems that this shock effect may also be produced by the opposite approach, by making the vocabulary perfectly banal and casual, as factual as a police report, in the manner of Valery Larbaud, for example, in "Images."

13. "Two Ages" in *The Ventriloquist's Doll* (London: Cresset Press, 1943).
14. (London: Faber & Faber, 1933).
15. Blaise Cendrars, *Le Panama ou Aventures de mes sept oncles* (Paris: Gallimard, 1919).
16. *Poètes d'Aujordhui*, Vol. 5.

> Un matin, à Rotterdam, sur le quai des Boompjes
> (C'était le 18 septembre 1900, vers huit heures)....[17]

> [One morning at Rotterdam, on the Boomjes quai
> (It was September 18, 1900, about eight o'clock)....]

Or Henry Reed who, in his collection *A Map of Verona*,[18] gives poems titles which are names of military exercises; in "Naming of Parts" he depicts soldiers learning the nomenclature of the parts of their weapons. Another banality to which the press generally is given is that childish and conventional morality which is parodied in the well-known poem "Passerelle du commandant," typified by phrases such as this:

> Il faut être chaste pour être bon

> [One must be chaste to be good]

and which ends with the magnificent line:

> Il faut être deux pour être trois.[19]

> [One must be two to be three.]

Then too we have observed in passing some unexpected forms: the cascade of verbs in Kipling's poem, omission of punctuation or capitalization, the disconnection of words in some lines, or again a heterodox ordering of the typography. In fact there is no longer any universally accepted form, because everything else is subordinated to effect. This is the very motto of industrial activity. Only the end result, the finished product, is important. Modern technique therefore molds poetry and discovers new metaphors for it which are capable of exciting our jaded tastes. Notice, for example, the form which E. E. Cummings employs in "she being Brand" to depict the behavior of his new automobile, economizing on all the capital letters, even that of the "I," with

17. *Poésies de A. O. Barnabooth.*
18. (New York: Reynal & Hitchcock, 1947).
19. Benjamin Péret, "Passerelle du commandant" in *Le Grand Jeu* (Paris: Gallimard, 1928).

the single exception of the one designating the automobile
itself, that new goddess.

> she being Brand
>
> -new;and you
> know consequently a
> little stiff i was
> careful of her and(having
>
> thoroughly oiled the universal
> joint. . . .[20]

Here we have an example of effects obtained solely by con-
trivances of form; other poets prefer to create new metaphors
and thus give renewed life to concepts which are rich but
stereotyped, like that of the heart:

> arc distendu de mon coeur machine à écrire pour les
> étoiles[21]

[distended bow of my heart typewriter for the stars]

or of death:

> Mais déja la mort s'avancait derrière nous,
> avec ses semelles en caoutchouc.[22]

[But already death was advancing behind us
on rubber-soled shoes.]

or simply by giving new interest to a commonplace action.
In a poem by Franz Hellens, for example, taking a rest becomes "dévisser ma fatigue."[23]

These are all instances of the modern molding of poetic
form. From the aesthetic point of view the magic spark
is always obtained by the clash of the traditional conception
with modern form. In the work of the American poet the

20. *The Oxford Book of American Verse.*
21. Tristan Tzara, "Maison Flake" in *Poètes d'aujourd'hui*, Vol. 32.
22. Paul Morand, "Paradiso-Belvédère" in *Poèmes.*
23. "Amis carrés étroits," *Anthologie de la N.R.F.*

suggestion is purely mechanical, composed of the jolting rhythm of the new machine being used roughly. Taylor's industrial time and motion studies are here applied to the traditional process of imitative harmony. The French poets force the allegorical image into a modern idiom. Cupid has a typewriter and the Grim Reaper rubber soles (if we think of Holbein's engravings, we realize how picturesque the image is).

Sometimes procedures for attaining the shock of surprise are so original as to defy classification. There is, to begin with, the method of telescoping to which English lends itself so well—for example, the phrase, "A Grief Ago," with which Dylan Thomas expresses grief's permanent impression on time by evoking the sorrow before the one which he is presently suffering.[24] Similarly, Paul Eluard stamps out this technicolor image: "Ta chevelure d'oranges. . ."[25] and Cendrars catches in a noose of three words the restrictive bleakness of a prisoner's existence: "Ta vie circoncise."[26] At the extreme limit of this method we have the infinite nuances of delicate play on words, from the simple punning on musical analogies in Apollinaire's "Cordes et concordes" or Max Jacob's "Chemin de nuit, nuit de chemin" to the pure word play of Jacob's "Comme un bateau":

> Comme un bateau le poète est âgé
> Ainsi qu'un dahlia, le poème étagé
> Dahlia! Dahlia que Dalila lia.[27]

and including the pun elaborated by Robert Desnos in "Les quatre sans cou"[28] ("faire les quatre cents coups" being the phrase for incorrigibly "sowing wild oats").

24. *The Collected Poems of Dylan Thomas* (New York: New Directions, 1953).
25. *Capitale de la Douleur* (Paris: Gallimard, 1926).
26. *Le Panama ou Aventures de mes sept oncles.*
27. *Le Laboratoire central.*
28. *Poètes d'aujourd'hui*, Vol. 16.

In all these methods there is perhaps something forced or contrived; for this reason Louis MacNeice, weary of the constant effort expended in writing that seldom came to life, returns to the simple cliché with melancholy homage:

> With all this clamour for progress
> This hammering out of new phrases and gadgets, new
> > trinkets and phrases
> I prefer the automatic, the reflex, the cliché of
> > velvet. . . .[29]

If the cliché is a metaphor which has lost the attraction and the novelty of surprise, it has gained the comfort of habit, and it passes unnoticed. The most moving poetry is perhaps that in which form seems to yield to substance with the ethereal simplicity that disappeared with Racine. We are forced to admit that today's poets, like our machines, prefer to strike hard and with precision.

The last category of surprise, which is especially effective because the modern reader is generally unprepared for it, is the metaphysical shock. To be sure, there is usually no long philosophical development involved, but rather the pronounciation of a few "profound" words deemed capable of confronting the reader with a great theme. For example, Roger Allard tries to exploit the concept of the unknown in his title "Blessures de guerre et d'ailleurs,"[30] and Valery Larbaud, that of nothingness in "Le Don de soi-même," which contains the following lines:

> Je rencontre toujours,
> Hors de moi comme en moi,
> L'irremplissable Vide,
> L'inconquérable Rien.[31]

> [I am always meeting
> Outside as well as within myself

29. "Homage to Clichés" in *Poems, 1925-1940*.
30. *Anthologie des Poètes de la N.R.F.*, p. 42.
31. *Poésies de A. O. Barnabooth*.

> The unfillable Void
> The unconquerable Nothing.]

The existentialists probably would not disavow the inspiration of such lines.

It is of interest, by the way, to notice William Plomer utilize in his poem "Father and Son: 1939" a method of description based on simultaneity similar to that of Dos Passos or Sartre's *Les Chemins de la liberté*, though the events in the poem happen miles apart:

> On a Sunday in September there were deck-chairs in
>   the sun,
> There was argument at lunch between the father and
>   the son
> (Smoke rose from Warsaw) for the beef was under-
>   done
> (Nothing points to heaven now but the anti-aircraft
>   gun)[32]

And we owe to Aldous Huxley a perfectly metaphysical poem based on a "surprise at being alive" worthy of Pascal, Maine de Biran, or Sartre. These are the first two stanzas of his "Fifth Philosopher's Song":

> A million million spermatozoa,
>   All of them alive:
> Out of their cataclysm but one poor Noah
>   Dare hope to survive.
>
> And among that billion minus one
>   Might have chanced to be
> Shakespeare, another Newton, a new Donne—
>   But the One was Me.[33]

Finally, in addition to simultaneity and the surprise of being, an ever-recurring third theme is that of time. In

32. *The Dorking Thigh.*
33. *Leda* (London: Chatto & Windus, 1920).

"East Coker" T. S. Eliot develops conceptions similar to those found in Valéry's "La Jeune Parque," but notice with what power of shock, what brutality from the very start of the poem.

In my beginning is my end.

And further on we seem to plumb the metaphysical gulf with these two sibylline lines:

And what you own is what you do not own
And where you are is where you are not.[34]

Thus it seems clear that the machine age has not produced a purely pragmatic, mechanized poetry. A two-fold influence has operated, in the usage of vocabulary as well as in the handling of themes, which has tended toward precision even on the metaphysical level, and has reduced sentimental vagueness.

This precision, far from being incompatible with poetry, strengthens it. There is much more than a truism born of English romanticism in Keats' famous observation:

"Beauty is truth, truth beauty,"—that is all
Ye know on earth, and all ye need to know.

The mystical communion indispensable to poetic expression can be secured only by truth. By "truth" we must understand not correspondence to a superficial mode of thinking which is currently in fashion, but a realization of the profound tendencies of the sensibility confronted by the exterior world. Clearly this is reserved only for a minority, and without going so far as to draw the romantic parallel of the poet-prophet or the poet-seer, we must admit that the double role in which we have found the poet of the machine—exalting and warning—offers fascinating analogies with the lofty notions of the last century.

Jean Cocteau underlies the elusive nature of poetry while trying to define its position in the modern world: "A creature

34. *Four Quartets.*

inhabiting another world and able to observe our own would laugh at science and at the machines we consider prodigious. This creature would know that science advances from one error to another and that machines paralyse our hands and our soul. But it would not be able to laugh at poetry, because poetry escapes analysis, and if I am certain that it is indispensable, I always ask myself, to what end. It is this enigmatic role that earns poetry its primacy in the world. . . ."[35] And by "enigmatic" Cocteau refers to the poem's roots in the deep, unchartered layers of our mind.

These poetic attitudes are not in the least new ones. They are permanent patterns of literary aesthetics. All authors of epics have assumed the task of exalting. Some, starting with the present, have anticipated the future with all the mysteries and potential dangers which it involves—these are the visionaries. Still others have humbly accepted the facts of reality such as they are, controlling their anxiety and forcing themselves to discover the maximum pleasure possible by the process of experience, though they remain incapable of escaping altogether the melancholy which proceeds from comparing reality to their ideal of a Golden Age. These attitudes correspond to three characterological types: the realistic, the imaginative, and the sentimental.

Only these last are able to retain a certain spiritual autonomy in our age. Their instinctive naïveté is their shield because their principal tendency is to becloud what is disagreeable. Thus they are saved through constant variations on the Cinderella legend. But because the consequence of dynamic force is inevitably to transcend reality and attain what can be imagined (we can see in present-day industry the irresistible impulse of progress) and, conversely, because so-called "pure" imagination is quickly outstripped by reality (F. L. Lucas justly writes, speaking of the Italian surrealist

35. "Lettre-Préface" in Paul Ginestier, ed., *Les Meilleurs Poèmes anglais et américains d'aujourd'hui, anthologie bilingue* (Paris: SEDES, 1958).

poet, "What Marinetti dreamed, Hitler did"[36]), the realist and the man of imagination necessarily merge in a unique kind of synthesis. And then a great spiritual effort becomes imperative. As Etienne Souriau says, "Reality is there . . . at the extreme limit of the effort of realization. Only there can existence be tasted and possessed."[37]   Only through this sort of higher existence, achieved through great effort, can the poet attain to the arcana of reality.

However, a possible source of difficulty is the problem of communication. Today's poet is—with infrequent exceptions —a spectator who evokes his emotions for other spectators. He depicts the work of a miner without being a miner and with the hope of interesting readers who by and large are not miners. Would that not seem, in principle, to prejudice the sincerity of the emotion and therefore its likelihood of being shared?   The answer is important because if it is an affirmative, most poetical themes on the industrial effort, except for those touching vast communities of men with the same interests, are invalidated.   Nevertheless we must admit that labor can be more readily appreciated from the sidelines, as illustrated by the old joke: "I adore work.   I can watch someone work for hours."   And it is no less true that work nowadays seizes upon the individual and occupies him too completely for him to be able to step back and observe himself objectively.   Besides, even if he succeeded in becoming enthusiastic over his own work, he would have only a partial and unrelated, hence unpoetic, view.   The soldier rarely grasps the strategic pattern of the battle in which he takes part.   We marvelled earlier at the landing of a great transatlantic plane, but the pilot was much too busy watching his instruments and guiding his machine to have the leisure to

36. F. L. Lucas, *op. cit.*, p. 137.

37. Quoted by R. Bayer in *Mélanges d'esthétique et de science de l'art offerts à Etienne Souriau* (Paris: Nizet, 1952), p. 38.   See also *Les Différents Modes d'existence* (Paris: Presses Universitaires de France, 1943).

experience such feelings. Of course this does not exclude the possibility that he may express the joy of his work after the event, as St.-Exupéry did, but at that moment he really ceases to be an actor and becomes a competent spectator.

It happens too that the modern poet who is aware of his role may be a voluntary witness of the event he plans to celebrate. Instead of making a mere objective report, he creates a poem which may be very moving if the subject is well chosen. James Kirkup, for example, was permitted to attend an operation by a great surgeon to whom he dedicated a poem in eighteen stanzas, entitled "A Correct Compassion." The dedication runs: "To Mr. Philip Allison, after watching him perform a Mitral Stenosis Valvulotomy in the General Infirmary at Leeds," and here are two illustrative lines:

> You with a curious nervous elegance laid bare
> The root of life, and put your finger on its beating
>   heart.[38]

It is striking to find the expression of the spectator sometimes unite with that of the actor. Georges Duhamel, who was a surgeon, writes in a story called "Le Dernier": "Remember, Rossignol, that I've held your heart, slippery and sinewy as a fish, in my hands."[39] The mystery that our mechanical civilization seemed to destroy is rediscovered at the very center of the temple of life.

*
* *

Now we come to the problem of catharsis or psychic release. Poetry's *raison d'être* is to satisfy some of our most secret urges. Dreaming as an intellectual activity is as useful to a well-balanced life as physical sport. Beauty manifests itself in the harmony of a disinterested action. The poetry

38. *A Correct Compassion* (London: Oxford University Press, 1952). This poem first appeared in *The Listener*, July 4, 1951, after having been read on the Third Programme of the B.B.C.

39. Cited in *La Pesée des âmes* (Paris: Mercure de France, 1949), p. 366.

of the machine effects the transference of dreaming into the current of life, giving it a new value. At a time when the various metaphors of flight began to seem used up and to become clichés, the ideas were renewed by the airplane and the aerodrome. Now the poet is able to express his joy of success. Through his expression he has achieved man's liberation from the Icarus complex, his feeling of being unable to effect "the unification of the force which moves and the object which is moved."[40]

Through the poetry of industrial effort, man will be able to recover from that psycho-pathology of failure which characterizes our age.[41] This does not mean that we think it necessary to change the archetypes of human imagination. No doubt a slow evolution is being accomplished, but we feel it would be unreasonable to hope for sudden changes. As we have shown, the poetry of our age tends really to actualize these archetypes. Not only are they no longer to be repressed or ignored, but they must be allowed to flourish with even greater liberty in the epic of modern technology. Man has always dreamed of being able to do certain things which are now in his power to perform, fly with the speed of sound, dive like a fish, etc. But he still has within him a complex of impotence which for milleniums has been stratified in his race, and it is poetry's task to free him from it. Through poetry we can participate in the joy of building and re-shaping the universe. But poetry must not only lead us on; in some cases it must hold us back. At bottom every catharsis has a double function: to reveal the possibilities of health and to combat sickness.

Our society is sick, too, because it assumes perfection. To be sure, metaphysics based on the absolute is one of man's needs, as P. Masson-Oursel has shown,[42] but to expect the

40. Bachelard, *L'Air et les songes*.

41. Dr. René Laforgue, *La Psycho-pathologie de l'échec* (Paris: Payot, 1944).

42. P. Masson-Oursel, *Le Fait métaphysique* (Paris: Presses Universitaires de France, 1941).

absolute is a real spiritual vice and a source of perpetual frustration. Yet this is too often an unconscious fault of the modern world which the poet is bound to unmask. We have seen that he has not shirked that duty. By constant recasting of mythological Hell, he shows us the Nemesis latent in our mechanized society. Like a psychiatrist, he offers not only a warning, but the opportunity of a cure. Thus a double movement of the poet's relation to society can be drawn; joy pulls him away, and catharsis draws him back. And this double tendency corresponds exactly to the psychology of work. Joy in the creation, then the depression of fatigue; power, then satiety; the solidity of earth, the fantasy of water, then disgust with the muck which results from their mixture. Life, which develops between two lost paradises, is always the dialectic of that greatest adventure which transcends them both, our birth.

It seems, then, that modern poetry, the poetry of the machine, is profoundly justified. When Gleb Struve affirms, "It has become a truism to say that poetry nowadays, in our modern world, is on the decline,"[43] he is no doubt repeating a common opinion, but one which is distorted because it turns on a confusion between quality and quantity. No doubt the poet's place in society seems to have been reduced, and poetry is printed in very small editions—although this is a relative matter and the enormously augmented volume of published material falsifies the comparison—but this does not necessarily prove a decline. First of all we must note that in a certain measure we are returning to the recitation of poetry which characterized the age of the troubadours. A poem printed in a small edition and read on the radio or rendered in a film will count its audience in the millions; and recordings of poetry read by the poets themselves or by professional actors have had phenomenal sales since the development of the microgroove record. All this is far from

43. Gleb Struve, *Soviet Russian Literature* (London: Routledge, 1935), p. 165.

negligible and perhaps constitutes a return to the true sense of the poetic message.   In addition poetry, in the wake of technical revolutions, has become aware of the fragility of formal traditions and is today freer than ever before, so clear of prejudices that it can even adapt itself to a strictly classical prosody, if that is necessary to the idea.   The substance of poetry, after being violently shaken by the surrealist crisis, has once more gained contact with the great realities of the human adventure whose aspects, often far from simple, it strives to represent.   "Man today is both Minotaur and Sphinx.   He is leaving the labyrinth; he is in quest of his own secret."[44]

There is, of course, a psychic danger in this.   According to Freud, there is much in common between the poet and the neurotic, and there is a pathetic unanimity of opinion on the fact that our world is neurotic.[45]   This observation could lead to developments as dangerous as they are facile, and it would be a mistake to forget the astonishment of the surrealists when they found themselves disavowed by most psychiatrists who thought that the process of automatic writing, for example, arose from a misinterpretation of the doctrines of the Vienna School.

In fact the true poet has enough imagination to transcend time.   Like Paul Valéry, he understands that behind the standardized object which our civilization offers lie "the countless experiments which one day reach the ideal and stop there.   Thousands of trials by thousands of men converge slowly toward the most economical and certain form . . . and millions of copies respond forever to the myriad previous gropings and cover them over."[46]   Anatole France has written a glowing tribute to these unknown thousands responsible for humanity's progress in *Le Livre de Mon Ami*:

44. Marcel Jean and Arpad Mezei, *Genèse de la pensée moderne* (Paris: Corrêa, 1950), p. 126.
45. Karen Horney, *The Neurotic Personality of our Time* (New York: W. W. Norton & Co., 1937).
46. *Eupalinos* (Paris: Gallimard, 1944), p. 99.

O my ancestor, in the unsoundable past in which you repose, receive the tribute of my gratitude, for I know how much I owe you. I know that your efforts have spared me many afflictions. . . . An obscure ideal drove you toward what is beautiful and good for all men . . . and that life, which you had received so frightful, you handed down a little less evil to your children. They labored in their turn to make it better. . . . They all exercised their ingenuity, and the continual effort of so many minds through the ages has produced marvels which embellish life. And every time that they invented an art or founded an industry, by that very act, they gave birth to moral beauties and created virtues.[47]

Through industrial effort this passage is inscribed in the dialectic of the world of imagination, and this composite is no doubt the equivalent, in poetry, of the law of universal gravitation, that is, a far-reaching discovery which solves for a time the innumerable problems in a particular subject. After the inhuman harshness of the industrial revolution which is coming to a close, the poets of the machine are reintroducing the most profound and poetic humanism in a civilization in which we were beginning to lose hold because the speed of its progress made it lose touch with the profound realities of life. The poets of the machine are still poorly understood. They are struggling in shadows, but they are secretly preparing the advent of a new genius, a Newton of poetry, to whom the glowing couplet by Pope will apply:

Nature, and Nature's Laws lay hid in Night.
God said, *Let Newton be!* and All was *Light*.

47. *Le Livre de mon ami* (Paris: Calmann-Lévy, 1926), p. 109.

Index of Authors Cited

Index of Authors Cited